The Impact of Ethnic Diversity in the Workplace: An Exploratory, Qualitative Inquiry on the Experience of African-American Employees in LMX Out-Groups

by

Larry D. Parker, Jr., Ph.D.

Copyright© 2016 / 2019

A Dissertation Presented in Partial Fulfillment of the Requirements for the Degree of Doctor of Philosophy, Capella University, Sept. 2016

Author	Larry D. Parker, Jr., Ph.D.
Publisher	DBC Publishing, Sandston / Richmond, VA
ISBN #s	ISBN-13: 978-1-948149143 ISBN-10: 1-948149141
Cover Art	2019© DBC Publishing

This text has been altered in format from the original dissertation to conform to better readability for the general-public and commercial publishing standards. The author may also have updated text, content, added more resources and bibliography material after the original dissertation was first published. Scholars reviewing the contents and formatting for thesis or dissertation styling should *not* use this book's current *formatting* as a model. Please see your educational institution's established dissertation guidelines for the acceptable formatting for the graduate level thesis for research reporting.

You may contact the author with questions, comments, or continuing research inquiries at: ldparkerjr@gmail.com

Table of Contents

List of Tables

List of Figures

Abstract

The purpose of this exploratory qualitative inquiry was to understand the personal experience of the African-American subordinate employee in the out-group of the Leader-Member Exchange (LMX) dyadic relationship and to gain insight into how such employees view themselves and their working relationships. The data analysis identified 12 themes within the responses of the participants. This research supported assertions that the low-quality relationships developed within the leader-member dyads had negative impacts on the individuals within the out-group. The existing literature focused heavily on members of the in-group, identifying the benefits of being inside the in-group.

The findings of this research confirmed the existence of the negative conditions of low-quality dyads. This study adds to the existing body of findings that support the existence of negative attributes of the LMX relationship and rate them as low quality. This research study adds to the literature on the factors

potentially contributing to the existence of low-quality
LMX relationships. This study also contributes to the
limited known narrative of the African-American
employee existing in the LMX out-group. This study
adds to the field of organization and management by
presenting an African-American subordinate out-
group narrative that identified factors that supervisors
can address to potentially strengthen the leader-
member dyad of demographically diverse workforces.
The improvement in leader-member dyad in
accordance with the LMX theory literature may
facilitate an improvement in the effectiveness of the
dyad in addressing organizational objectives.

The themes of this research provide potential
constructs upon which further research can build to
develop the understanding of out-groups and the
impacts of diversity.

Dedication and Acknowledgments

This book is dedicated to God, my family and friends. I owe everything I am and will ever achieve to you.

Larry D. Parker, Jr., Ph.D.

Dedication and Acknowledgements

This book is dedicated to God, my family and friends. Whatever thing I am and will ever amount to comes from me.

Larry D. Pastor, Jr., PhD

CHAPTER 1

INTRODUCTION

Introduction to the Problem

The population of the United States was likely to increase in ethnic diversity over the next three decades; 2010-2040 (Humes, Jones, & Ramirez, 2011). Research has indicated an increase in ethnic diversity may negatively impact the management relationships of the workforce (Avery, Lerman, & Volpone, 2010). The meta-analytical work of Pettigrew and Tropp (2006) provided evidence that well-structured contact with individuals of other racio-ethnic groups can lessen prejudice – in some situations. Research findings also suggested the interaction of diverse racio-ethnic groups produced stress, anxiety, and discomfort for individuals involved (Dovidio, Hebl, Richeson, & Shelton, 2006).

The minorities of these racio-ethnic groups were concerned, during times that they were forced to interact with those within the majority racio-ethnic group, that they would experience prejudice and/or encounter confirmation of negative racio-ethnic stereotypes. The individuals within the majority racio-ethnic group were afraid of seeming prejudiced, and/or finding any negative stereotypes they may hold of minorities may have been true (Richeson & Shelton, 2007). An increase in the minority population in the United States potentially could increase the interactions of individuals of different racio-ethnic backgrounds.

The demographic composition of the U.S. workforce was rapidly changing. The U.S. Census Bureau reported in 2010, minorities comprised 38% of the U.S. population (Humes et al., 2011). The projected population changes will have resulted in half the labor force coming from racio-ethnic minorities by 2050 (Avery et al., 2010). This reflected two forces: the mortality of immigrants and the birth patterns of major ethnic groups. First, current immigration policy favors allowing working-age adults to immigrate and to start a family in the United States. Second, some ethnic groups grow at different rates depending upon the racio-ethnic group's fertility and mortality

(Shrestha & Heisler, 2011). The projected increase in minority representation in the workforce by 2040 will have increased the frequency with which managers and their direct subordinates will interact. The increased possibility of ethnic diversity between managers and their direct subordinates may increase the number of employees with low-quality management relationships and adversely affect organization effectiveness (Avery et al., 2010).

Background of the Study

The initial Leader-Member Exchange (LMX) research was mostly quantitative in nature. The LMX research focused primarily on the impact the relationships had on the work attitudes of subordinates. Liden and Graen (1980) substantiated the impact that leadership approach had on subordinate productivity, communication, and interaction effectiveness. Graen and Uhl-Bien (1995) further advanced the theory of LMX research, which asserted that leadership effectiveness occurred when leaders and their subordinates created relationships that matured and positively affected leadership. The leaders and organizations they represented would

benefit from the work effectiveness that mature and
positive relationships produced (Graen & Uhl-Bien,
1995). Graen and Uhl-Bien identified the existence
and formation of in-groups and out-groups.

As knowledge of organizational management
and leadership theories developed and evolved over
the years, researchers delved deeper into how the
different factors that created the in-groups and out
groups affected leadership (Graen & Uhl-Bien, 1995).
Graen and Uhl-Bien deemed trust a significant
influence on leadership, because in it, some found
"assurance in the integrity and ability of the other
person" (Walker, 2011, p. 2). The research on how
diversity impacts trust was limited. Although de
Cremer, van Dijke, and Bos (2006) found that
consistent demonstration of personal integrity by a
leader would develop trust within the leader-follower
relationship, it was not clear what goes through the
mind of the African-American employees in the out-
groups within these organizations. There was a lack
of qualitative assessments in research, which would
have provided insight into the reason that factors that
previous studies had highlighted had the effects they
did on leadership dyads.

Statement of the Problem

Although there have been studies of leadership
development and diversity, many have been
quantitative in nature, validating the impact of
diversity on leadership. Research of a qualitative
nature is necessary to address the lack of knowledge
of the personal experiences of minority employees
negatively affected by increased diversity. This study
explored the personal experiences of African-
American subordinate employees in the out-groups of
their Caucasian supervisors as defined by LMX
theory. This study provided an opportunity to address
a gap in the knowledge of a theory of organizational
management and leadership: leader-member
exchange (LMX). The gap in the literature was
specifically about qualitative research and the lack of
personal perspectives of the minority within the LMX
out-group (Amogbokpa, 2010).

Purpose of the Study

The purpose of this exploratory, qualitative inquiry was to gain a greater understanding of the personal experiences of African-American subordinate employees in the out-groups of the LMX dyadic relationship and to gain insight into how they view themselves and their working relationships. This study defined diverse demographic as the ethnic difference between the manager and the employee. This research study investigated the perspectives of African-American subordinate employees in the LMX out-groups of their Caucasian supervisors and identified factors that were perceived to have enhanced or detracted from the development of the professional relationship.

Rationale

An exploratory, qualitative-inquiry method of research coupled with the LMX theory were deemed appropriate for investigating the perspectives of the subordinate participants experiencing an ethnically-diverse, supervisor-subordinate relationship. Through exploratory qualitative inquiry, the individual accounts were deduced to themes and coded through interpretive methods (Androff, 2010). The dynamic and intangible nature of relationships was difficult to measure with quantitative methods. The essence of the experience was more accurately captured using an exploratory, qualitative-inquiry approach, which did not restrict participants in personal descriptions of their experiences (Androff, 2010). The best way to describe and analyze the relationship between the leader and member was by using LMX theory as a basis for discussion. The constructs of LMX theory was observable, and researchers were able to assign the constructs to a position on the leadership effectiveness continuum identified by Dansereau, Graen, and Haga (1975).

Research Question

ResQ: How do African-American subordinate employees within the out-groups of their Caucasian immediate supervisors, as defined by the LMX theory, describe their leader-member, dyad narratives?

Significance of the Study

The significance of the research grows in
relevance as the demographic makeup of the U.S.
workforce changes to a greater minority
representation (Avery et al., 2010). This study may
contribute to more effective management of a diverse
employee population by building upon existing
management relationship research and expanding the
LMX theory. This study may also contribute to the field
of organization and management due to the
increasing significance of diversity within the U.S.
workforce.

The research of cultural diversity and its impact
in the workplace was largely the work of Hofstede
(1984). However, the primary basis of Hofstede's work
was national traits identified by six dimensions, which
Hofstede used to assess relationships internationally.
The Globe Project expanded the six dimensions of
culture identified by Hofestede to nine (House,
Hanges, Javidan, Dorfman, & Gupta, 2004).

Although the Globe Project elicited more
personal values of the participant, the study was

limited in nature, and only looked at the experience
using an international and national paradigm. The
research study was extensive, covered over 62
countries, and interviewed over 17,300 middle
managers. The study had implications that contributed
to organization theory, motivation theory, and
leadership. A major finding of the study was that
cultural dimensions did have an influence on leaders
(House et al., 2004).

Andresen (2007) further asserted the
categorization within the Globe Project included
cultural dimensions such as internal, external, and
organizational dimensions. This study qualitatively
assessed the ethnic differences identified within
Andresen's research on internal and external
dimensions. The findings of earlier research studies
were limited in application to local geographic areas
due to the national and international constructs of the
cultural dimensions the researchers used as metrics.
This qualitative research study was not constrained
by those same constructs and facilitated the collection
personal perspectives on the dynamics of the diverse
relationship with management.

This research study's findings may provide leaders with information to improve the leader's interactions with a demographically diverse staff. This study focused on a population of subordinates with experience of being in the out-group of a diverse leader-member dyad. The conclusions may provide a foundation upon which researchers can merge social and behavioral-science research with leadership studies to achieve more effective and culturally-diverse global organizations.

Definition of Terms

Leader-member dyadic relationship: the interaction between single followers and their respective leaders (Bhal, Gulati, & Ansari, 2009).

Narrative: in-depth conversations that provide insight on oppressive experiences and dispute dismissive views of inequality (Delgado, 2000).

Dyad: A relationship consisting of two parts; leader and subordinate (Bhal, Gulati, & Ansari, 2009).

In-group: Members of an organization that receives more attention, the most rewards, and are managed informally. As a result, in-group members have higher productivity, job satisfaction, and motivation (Schriesheim, Neider, & Scandura, 1998).

Racio-ethnic group: A designation of similar individuals identified as sharing the same race and ethnic characteristics (Dovidio, Hebl, Richeson, & Shelton, 2006).

Out-group: Members of an organization that receives less attention, fewer rewards, and management by formal rules and policies. As a result, out-group members have lower productivity, job satisfaction, and motivation (Schriesheim, Neider, & Scandura, 1998).

Assumptions and Limitations

Assumptions

Theoretical assumption: Demographic diversity can affect LMX theory.

Topical assumptions: Individuals within the out-group of an LMX dyad have similar perspectives on their experiences.

Methodical assumptions: Explorative qualitative inquiry was the appropriate research method to identify the impact ethnic diversity had on a leader-member relationship.

Limitations

The limitations of the study fall into two categories: researcher experience and phone interviews.

Researcher experience: The researcher was new to the use of NVivo software. The researcher completed available NVivo software training to mitigate the lack of experience.

Phone interviews: The researcher's use of phone interviews limited the opportunity to observe body language responses to interview questions. The researcher utilized probing questions and allowed

ample time for participants to expound upon answers
to mitigate the lack of face-to-face interviews.

Nature of the Study (Conceptual Framework)

The conceptual framework for this study was
the Leader-Member Exchange (LMX) theory. Graen
and Uhl-Bien (1995) advanced LMX theory research
that asserted leadership effectiveness occurred during
the maturation of the relationship between leaders
and members who were their direct subordinates.
The LMX theory framework was utilized to evaluate
the narratives of the personal experiences of the
African-American subordinate employees within the
LMX out-groups of their immediate Caucasian
supervisors. The Venn diagram in Figure 1 illustrates
the theoretical and conceptual framework the
researcher used to explore the convergence of LMX
dyad members' experiences: leader, member (in-
group), member (out-group). The researcher expected
that – at the point of convergence – the experiences
of African-American subordinate employees within the
LMX out-groups of their immediate Caucasian
supervisors would need further analysis. Graen and

Uhl-Bien's narrative gives a perspective that few researchers have codified and analyzed. There was a gap in the literature on qualitative research pertaining to the lack of personal perspective of the minority within the LMX theory out-group (Amogbokpa, 2010). The literature review highlighted seminal and recent works serving as a basis for this study.

Conceptual Framework

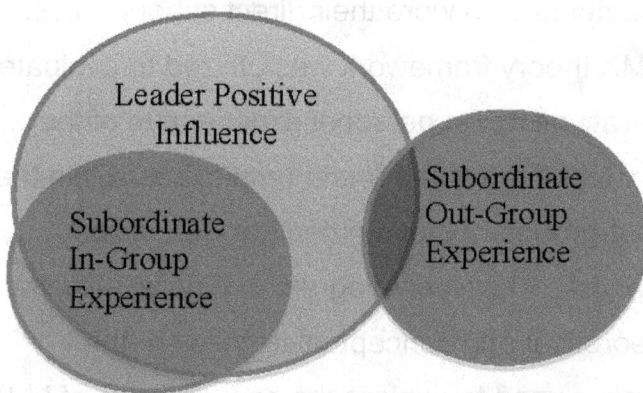

Supervisor LMX Positive Influence (Blue Sphere)

Figure 1 – Conceptual Framework

CHAPTER 2
LITERATURE REVIEW

Introduction

This chapter provided a review of seminal and current literature relevant to the problem proposed in Chapter 1. The conduct of comprehensive research included the review of literature peculiar to the research problem. The intent was to synthesize the current knowledge of the problem to develop a thorough understanding of the facts and any perceived research gaps.

The literature review included three areas: (a) the origin of LMX theory, (b) the maturation of LMX, and (c) a critical analysis of the concerns of LMX through the synthesis of LMX research design and constructs. The literature review contained only references reflecting significant research on the development and maturation of this leadership theory. The review included a synthesis of the various research approaches to LMX. This synthesis of findings highlights the knowledge gap that existed in this field of study.

Leader-Member Exchange Theory

Leader-Member Exchange (LMX) theory was a way of assessing the dyadic relationship between a leader and his or her subordinates (T. A. Scandura, Graen, & Novak, 1986). Although this description of LMX theory was an extreme simplification of the seminal works of T. A. Scandura et al. (1986), it made clear the researchers of the theory were making specific attempts to assess the effects and strengths of the relationship between the leader and immediate subordinates. The origin of LMX depends on which paradigm one chose to view the similarities of LMX to other leadership theories.

In this literature review, the researcher discussed the origin of LMX theory maturation, analysis, and metrics. Studies conducted since the conception of LMX theory utilized different analysis approaches and metrics. The lack of linear progression over the last four decades led to

academic reviews of the bodies of research on LMX.
These reviews generated observations that
characterized the strengths and weaknesses of the
LMX theory.

Origins of LMX

Opinions concerning the origins of LMX
depend upon the previous leadership theory to which
readers believed it was most akin. A review of the
literature of other scholars suggests attribution of the
early roots of LMX to the Vertical Dyad Linkage (VDL)
of the 1960s. Some social-sciences-based
researchers from the 1960s and later have argued
LMX developed from research into leadership themes
of reciprocity (Gouldner, 1960), social exchange
(Blau, 1964), similarity attraction (Byrne, 1971), and
relational roles (Katz & Kahn, 1978).

The concept of reciprocity was the universal
and critical factor of leadership theory (e.g., LMX).
The reciprocity norm was pervasive and universal
across cultures and relationships. This norm of
reciprocity asserted an individual in a formal
relationship was obliged to return favorable treatment

'in kind' for favorable treatment received (Gouldner, 1960). Research preceding LMX found leaders expected subordinates to reciprocate preferential treatment with efforts above the formal relationship contract (Lapierre & Hackett, 2007).

Blau (1964) found social exchange was not just an exchange between two individuals, but social exchange manifested into indirect lines of interaction when it was the norm of a group to feel an obligation to duplicate a deed-in-kind for one an individual had received. This concept was similar to the norms of reciprocity and may have been one of the tenets upon which LMX theory developed. Within the norms of social exchange, a subordinate felt an obligation to reciprocate a leader's favorable actions and trust through improved organizational performance (Gerstner & Day, 1997).

A number of researchers choose not to place the origin of LMX too far from previous bodies of leadership knowledge. These researchers stated LMX theory emerged from dyad research in the 1980s resulted from the Vertical Dyad Linkage Theory (VDL) model of leadership. The researchers of the VDL theory asserted there was a difference between relationships within work units. The premise of VDL suggested there was a significant relationship between leaders and followers. This aspect of the theory gave birth to LMX theory.

LMX focused on the dyadic relationship between the leader and follower with an emphasis on the changing quality of the relationship over time (Graen, Liden, & Hoel, 1982). This theory developed in contrast to the social psychology belief that leaders and followers did not share an interest and were unable to create informal relationships.

According to Katz and Kahn (1966), there were similarities between VDL and LMX theories. For example, in the VDL construct, each dyad forms a social exchange unit of analysis. Graen, Liden, and Hoel (1982) suggested relationships worked along a continuum and negotiating latitude affected the strength of the relationship. Members achieving the most successful relationship(s) likely had high-negotiating latitude associated with the in-group, and those members with poor negotiating latitude were associated with the out-group. Dienesch and Liden (1986) presented findings that argued LMX acted as a three-dimensional construct: perceived contribution to relationship, loyalty, and affect based on interpersonal attraction. This conceptualization of the construct later evolved into a four-dimensional construct as developed by Liden and Maslyn (1998). The four-dimensional construct, also known as Global LMX, measured the quality of the leader-member relationship with the following factors:

1. Affect – a measurement of the interpersonal affection for each other within the dyad.
2. Contribution – a measurement of the effort each member of the dyad extended towards the shared implicit and explicit goals of the dyad.
3. Loyalty – publicly expressed support by the leader and follower to the well-being of the other and their goals.
4. Professional Respect – the reputation the leader or follower developed within and outside of the organization of excelling in the respective profession. (Liden & Maslyn, 1998)

The growth of interest in leadership expanded the research findings on the effects of leadership influence on organizations and followers. Some

studies found leadership created a culture and climate
that facilitated innovation and creativity (Amabile,
Conti, Coon, Lazenby, & Herron, 1996; Mumford &
Gustafson, 1988). The leadership of an organization
had a significant influence on the manner in which a
follower or member of an organization went about
achieving goals or tasks (Redmond, Mumford, &
Teach, 1993). Redmond et al.'s (1993) research
findings suggested leaders' behaviors supported
problem solving and enhanced followers' self-efficacy,
which in turn facilitated innovation.

The Stages of Maturation: VDL to LMX

Like the origin of LMX, the evolution and
maturation of the theory did not have a linear path
from its origin to the present-day construct. The
approaches to the research were sometimes
conflicted, but there was a distinct enough
progression the concepts fell into stages. A
comprehensive review of the research place since the
introduction of LMX framed these four stages.

First Stage: Dyadic Focus

The first stage of the VDL concept maturing
beyond the original conceptual approach was when
researchers asserted leaders and subordinates
developed relationships unique to each subordinate.
The paradigm was a departure from the previous view
that leaders acted in a consistent manner toward all
subordinates. This approach was a departure from the
focus on the leader's actions and introduced the
dyadic focus. The name of this previous notion was
the Average Leadership Style (ALS) model.

Second Stage: Varied Dyad

This concept marked the second stage in the
maturation of LMX from VDL, in which different
relationships developed within the workplace. The
paradigm in the second stage dominated the majority
of LMX research. The unique leader-member
relationship construct was the basis of the detailed
analysis of the principles surrounding the LMX
construct. Although LMX research occurred over an

extended period since 1980, LMX had its roots in the paradigm and research approach of scholars during this period.

Third Stage: Organizational Influence

In the third stage, the dominant conceptual approach to dyadic research was the leadership-making model. The emphasis of this approach to dyadic study was the leader's differentiation of subordinates and how the leader interacted with each person on a one-to-one basis (Graen & Uhl-Bien, 1995). During this period, there was a research emphasis on where within the organization the leader-member dyadic relations developed and the degree of effectiveness. Although still placing emphasis on the relationship, scholars realized external factors may have played a part in the development of the relationship.

Fourth Stage: Dyad Grouping

The fourth stage of evolution of the LMX theory broadened the scope of the research from the single dyad to the larger group. This final stage explored the dyadic relationships of an organization within a larger organizational construct (Graen & Uhl-Bien, 1995). This research approach recognized similar leadership styles could work for different groups depending upon the construct of the organization.

Summary of the Four-Stage Model Maturation

Although the four-stage description appears to explain a linear development of the LMX leadership theory, the evolution has been anything but linear. The stages do not fall neatly into a pattern of points in time with beginning and ending dates of groupings of research. A better explanation would be a conglomeration of similar thoughts and approaches to dispersed research. Even the seminal researchers Graen and Uhl-Bien (1995) confirmed this assessment of the conduct of research within this model. Graen and Uhl-Bien (1995) themselves cited works in a non-linear fashion, further complicating the argument LMX was built upon established knowledge with a similar approach.

The lack of traditional growth of knowledge of

dyadic interactions made it difficult for researchers of
LMX to target and identify broadly-accepted findings
and assertions. The academic community noted these
observations. The LMX theory had been plagued with
a lack of consistency in its definitions of theory,
metrics, and analysis.

Observations of LMX Challenges

Although LMX has garnered a high level of
interest since its inception as a conceptual framework,
there seemed to be challenges, including fidelity of
the theory, metrics, and appropriateness of the
approach, to the research method. These three issues
outlined the weakness and strengths of LMX theory
as it matured from the VDL theory. To researchers, the
theory not being rigid was its strength, but a
discussion of this comes later in the literature review.

LMX Theory Fidelity

A researcher once stated a good theory was
the epitome of practicality. Scholars believe a good
theory has its basis in precise concepts and adequate

definitions within its assertions (Schriesheim, Castro,
& Cogliser, 1999). The LMX theoretical approach
presented assertions in a clear and organized manner
(Bacharach, 1989; Copi, 1954). The preciseness of a
theoretical foundation created the environment that
facilitated data-gathering and future collaborative
research to build upon other researchers' foundations.
When research was sound, it referenced the work of
previous researchers while simultaneously
contributing new work with clear links to previous
theories. The most significant of challenges was the
fidelity and completeness of the LMX theory
(Dienesch & Liden, 1986).

As the theoretical construct evolved from VDL
to LMX, there was a constant, but unpredictable,
evolution of assessed elements within the research. A
review of the theoretical constructs evolution since
1980, indicated the earliest elements of the VDL
studies were exploratory in nature and did not provide
details regarding theoretical foundations and further
definitions of the elements construct. Even the
seminal researchers in the first 10 years of LMX
theory did not always put forth a definition of the
theory in their respective research constructs (Graen,

Liden, & Hoel 1982). The Ohio State data-collection instrument showed the exploratory approach as a validation to provide metrics to assess different aspects of the theory. The use of this accepted tool was short-lived. As researchers embarked on new research and moved in a familiar direction for LMX research, researchers (1975) further developed the theoretical definition of LMX and laid the groundwork for the current approach (Graen & Cashman, 1975).

In 1976, Graen proposed the basis of the LMX theory construct was the quality of the exchange between the leader and subordinate with the three specific factors of confidence, interpersonal skill, and trust. Although supporting the dyadic approach, Cashman, Dansereau, Graen, and Haga (1976) saw the relationship between leaders and subordinates as more affected by attention and sensitivity. A year later Graen and Ginsburgh (1977) expanded the factors to the latest sub-dimension list that included support, reward, and satisfaction. It was then that researchers first described the elements as both the exchange between leaders and subordinates and leader acceptance.

In the late seventies, LMX factors expanded to include elements such as sensitivity, support, and attention. Researchers argued for the exclusion of trust from the elements of LMX. This consternation over the theoretical definitions of LMX continued for a decade. During the 1980s, Graen and other researchers further defined LMX as the quality of the didactic relationship between leaders and subordinates (later described as members). It was during the 1980s that parallel research began to describe the variance of the missions or content to the construct.

Although the work of LMX researchers generated development and structure, the maturation and validity of the research theory continued to be complicated by other researchers embarking on research with ever-expanding elements and metrics. A literature review of LMX theories in the late 1990s found over three dozen dissertations during the 1980s using approximately a dozen different theoretical definitions (Schriesheim, Castro, & Cogliser, 1999). These three dozen studies further complicated the advancement of knowledge because of the inability to build upon or confirm the work of the other. There were also differences in metrics and elements between studies.

It was not until Graen and Scandura (1987) provided their first approach to the three-phase model of LMX development: role taking, role making, and roll routinization that the first real, clear, and concise definition for LMX appeared in an article.

Leader-Member Exchange is (a) a system of components and their relationships, (b) involving both members of a dyad, (c) involving interdependent patterns of behavior, (d) sharing mutual outcome instrumentalities, and (e) producing conceptions of environments, cause maps, and value (T. A. Scandura et al., 1986, p. 580). Graen and Scandura (1987) also extended the next dimensions or elements to include influence latitude. In 1977, Scandura argued the LMX sub-domain included trust, sensitivity, support, and attention sub-dimensions. Over the years, Graen and Scandura proposed slightly altered sub-dimensions that included trust or, in some cases, excluded trust. In the 1980s, Graen and Scandura (1987) decided the definition of LMX would be the quality of the exchange between the leader and subordinate(s) while including sub-dimensions and sub-content of the construct.

Although research continued into the next decade (1990s), there was little focus on the construct of LMX. Lack of consistency and definition and even the content of the elements of the theory construct did not facilitate effective research by scholars during this period. This research approach was apparent even in different works by the same authors during the 1990s. The inconsistency of the sub-content of the construct continues, but more recent studies have explained the phenomenon as the quality of the exchange between a leader and subordinate(s). Other definitions included the construct of negotiating latitude or supervisor tension, social exchange relationships, the maturity of the relationship, negotiating latitude, incremental influence, and individual leadership (Yammarino & Dubinsky, 1990).

Summary of LMX Theory Maturation

The development of the LMX theory has been dynamic throughout the 40 years since its inception in 1980. The roots of the theory lie in sociological constructs such as research studies in reciprocity and leadership theories focused on VDLs. The literature loosely defined LMX theory until 1986.

It was common for researchers over the approximate past four decades (1980-2019) to use variations in the dimensions and sub-dimensions they used as constructs. This researcher commonality may have had an effect on the dyad between the leader and member. There were constant, inexplicable changes to the research instruments noted in studies. These constant changes, apparently without adhering to the scholarly principles of testing, created weaknesses and invalidity in LMX research. The approach of researchers during this period also lacked discipline to facilitate practices that built upon previous research.

LMX Metrics

Another important aspect of valid research was the metric that researchers chose to measure the phenomenon of interest. Psychological measurement is in itself an area of study that garners scrutiny. The study of such intangible aspects of interactions and/or emotions required adherence to strict established criteria by previous researchers. Changes to scale ranges or dimensions must have theoretical justifications, supported with evidence of the need for and results of the changes (Schriesheim et al., 1999).

Researchers in the field of leadership theory noted a lack of attention to the psychometric aspects of research (Barge & Schlueter, 1991; Schriesheim & Kerr, 1997). The fidelity of measurement was not a matter of convenience; it was an academic requirement for assertions within the leadership body of knowledge for scholars in other areas to view as valid for acceptance. Researchers identified and accepted principles of scale development others have developed and validated (Hinkin, 1995; Nunally & Bernstein, 1994). The acceptance of established practices in the measurement of psychometrics enhanced the chances of research receiving favorable peer review. The discipline of maintaining consistency of measurement of elements or dimensions was a significant challenge for researchers of LMX theory.

As researchers struggled or refused to define LMX theory as they conducted early research on the evolution of the theory, those same researchers also varied what they deemed significant for the psychometrics (Portugal & Yukl, 1994). Issues resulted from LMX's theoretical leader also varied as his stance on the metrics noted as the focus of study. It was significant to note that Graen, one of the seminal researchers, found value in the flexibility to change elements when measuring phenomena throughout the evolution of the theory. Graen offered no theoretical support for doing so beyond the assertion elements had an effect on the dyad, on which his study focused. This approach to changing the scale without theoretical support or justification ran counter to Nunally and Bernstein's (1994) argument for disciplined scale development and management. Graen either published or co-authored studies within the same year that utilized varied data elements and data-collection tools.

If the academic community had a reason for concern about the validity of some of this work, these concerns were understandable per the inconsistency and lack of a common paradigm in Graen's approach. It is important to researchers to use validated research methods so the academic community will accept the analyses and conclusions. Although the conceptual approach varied greatly from VDL to LMX, there was also a concern for the development of research through the stages of LMX theory. It would be an inaccurate perception that Graen and Uhl-Bien's (1995) research asserted or conveyed LMX progressed in an orderly manner through the four stages to develop to the present model of leadership theory. Graen and Uhl-Bien (1995), both seminal researchers of LMX, routinely utilized elements and findings from various stages or conglomerations of thought within the same analysis. Therefore, Graen and Uhl-Bien debunked the concept that LMX developed chronologically.

For more specific examples of how varied the metrics researchers have utilized within LMX have been since its inception, several data points from the comprehensive review of LMX research covering a 30-year period by Schriesheim et al. (1999) outlined how prevalent was the lack of psychometric discipline. Over 40 years since, the LMX construct utilized a different measurements and scales to assess anywhere from two to 25 elements (Dienesch & Liden, 1986; Weitzel & Graen, 1989).

The early research on LMX utilized a tool from Ohio State research called the Leader Behavior Description Questionnaire (LBDQ). Air Force-sponsored researchers developed this tool in a study of leaders. It was a psychometric tool that met the rigor necessary for peer-reviewed research (Hinkin, 1995; Nunally & Bernstein, 1994).

In 1973, Graen, Dansereau, Minami, and Cashman utilized all 40 'consideration' and 'initiating' items of the tool as metrics. Instead of continuing to utilize the full tool, LMX researchers began either to utilize aspects of the tool selectively or to augment it with additional items. Graen et al. (1973) followed up their initial research by augmenting the LBDQ with 20 additional elements. The LMX research by Schriesheim and Kerr (1979) continued to alter the LBDQ further.

The early years of LMX research saw additional metric tools to the research studies. A review of the earliest metric tools indicated researchers adopted more than five tools to measure some aspects of leadership: Role Orientation Index, Leader-Member Influence, the Supervisory Attention Scale, Negotiating Latitude, and Leader Acceptance.

Each of these metrics took a paradigm approach to measuring the same dyad. Researchers measured the quality of the relationship from the leader's perspective and/or the perceptions of the followers in some studies. In other studies, differences in the scales were either additions or subtractions from a measured item.

The 1970s saw studies by the same researchers referencing the findings of other studies to support the use of an item or items within a scale for research. The majority of these specific citations were traceable to Schiemann (1977), within a literature review for his research. This nepotistic citation relationship of Schiemann's research weakened the argument for the validity of LMX research. As the 70s closed, researchers introduced four variants of previous scales into the body of knowledge. The published works did not explain the depth, extent of, or justifications for item changes.

The inexplicable changes in instruments to study LMX did not improve in the 1980s. A development did occur in the measurement of LMX theory by the creation of a seven-item scale by Graen, Novak, and Sommercamp (1982). This scale would foreshadow the LMX-7 scale by 15 years. LMX-7 became a more commonly used measure for LMX operationalization (Gerstner & Day, 1997). Studies now utilize the LMX-7 or a five-item LMX measure, with the five items varying between studies. Consistent with the drifting fidelity of the LMX measure over the previous decades (1980-2019), Graen and Uhl-Bien (1995) later recommended a revised seven-item metric to researchers. The new scale had similarities with the original seven elements, but the difference was in response categories. As with previous research development, lack of rationale for making the recommendations and changes to LMX-7 further exacerbated the confusion within the field of study. Graen and Uhl-Bien (1995) provided no rationale or adequate justification for the newly revised element scale. Schriesheim et al. (1999) noted even minor modifications to the scale changed the psychometric properties and supporting evidence of testing the revised measures with adequate peer review was needed.

Although evolving the psychometrics as new knowledge emerged about LMX theory was understandable, the number of changes and little

explanation of what the new scale measured raised
the question of the validity of previous findings.
Researchers used an additional 12 scales to measure
LMX through the remainder of the 1990s. The desire
to expand the LMX construct with such multidimensionality and quality of exchange meant the
advent of tools to assess sub-dimensions, including
subordinate contribution and loyalty (Dienesch &
Liden, 1986).

Summary of Metrics

The history of the LMX theory development
was filled with examples of researchers attempting to
expand knowledge, but not always devoting attention
to details regarding research discipline. There was a
departure from psychometric principles to pursue data
on personality sub-dimensions that academic
researchers perceived as impacting the LMX dyad.
The lack of justification for scale modification and
interpretation of meanings leaves little to support the
validity of research findings through the history of
LMX. One implication was the elimination of the
ability to follow researchers to duplicate their work

and understand the paradigm of the research
conducted when undertaking the analysis process.

The leader-member dyad had undergone
influence, both internal to the dyad and external. The
seminal researchers' approaches to metrics over the
46 years since its inception (1973-2019) had seemed
exploratory. Although there were attempts to build
upon the previous works of researchers, there were
limited chains of scientific rationale that researchers
can trace to support the changes in psychometric
scales.

LMX Analysis

It is important to establish and understand the
perspective by which a phenomenon was studied.
Organizations have multiple levels of sub-structures:
individuals, dyads, workgroups, and departments.
The researcher specifies where and at what level the
construct of interest should focus efforts as an initial
consideration for investigating the phenomenon within
the organizational structure. This allowed the
researcher to link metrics and analytical data tools to
the appropriate level of analysis. The theory, methods

of measurement, and data analytical technique should align throughout the research model to ensure the findings were appropriately addressing the research question (Klein, Dansereau, & Hall,1994). The approach level to analysis was a critical aspect of the design of any research. The VDL theory departed from the ALS approach and its focus on dyads as its hypothesized level of analysis. The VDL model was the initial treatment of leadership.

This was the focus of study at the dyadic level of analysis, which identified the dyad between the leader and one subordinate. The basis of the initial VDL model was the premise that a leader's interaction with subordinates was different with each subordinate. The VDL model was a departure from the ALS model, which had been dominant in earlier research (Kerr, Schriesheim, Murphy, & Stogdill, 1974).

This literature review of LMX yielded little evidence of discipline or motivation among researchers to define the theory. There was a lack of consistency in the scales and metrics researchers chose to evaluate LMX. The inconsistency did not transfer to the identification of the level of analysis for LMX research (Keller & Dansereau, 1995;

Schriesheim, Cogliser, & Neider, 1995). Despite concerns with the chronological research and development of the LMX theory and challenges in psychometrics, the researchers of LMX settled on the dyad of leader and member as the level of analysis for the theory. This identified level was that the seminal researchers expected the level effects to manifest and which they believed was best to measure (Graen, Liden, &Hoel, 1982)

That LMX researchers commonly accept this level of analysis was significant. This was a component of a researcher being able to build upon the previous work of researchers. While of researchers today make the assumption elements have a basis in the existence of a leadership style differentiating between subordinates within a workgroup, the most recent work by Graen and Uhl-Bien (1995) made a departure from the previous research with the assertion that LMX was strictly a relational concept. These researchers asserted the leader and subordinate dyad was no longer the primary focus of the elements. They saw the leader and subordinate dyad relationship as the main focus. Keller & Dansereau (1995) asserted the current conceptualization allowed for any level of analysis to achieve an appropriate relationship as long as the relationship itself remained the focus. Researchers suggested there needs to be further theoretical research regarding the level of analysis of elements.

Summary of LMX Analysis

The LMX theory had struggled with validity due to challenges researchers encountered with the fidelity of the theory definition and the adherence to principles of psychometrics. Researchers had unified the level of analysis for LMX as the dyad. This was a positive for future researchers to build upon previous findings. Although different approaches exist to measure the effects on the dyad, findings can support research that focused on the same level of analysis.

Gap in Knowledge

The evolution of VDL theory to LMX involved exploratory research that was wrought with challenges to using definitions and metrics. To understand the significance these challenges better and to identify potential improvements, it was necessary to review a key study in the early stages of VDL maturation. Acknowledged as one of the seminal researchers of the impact that cultural diversity had in the workplace, Hofstede (1984) developed research that inspired a research initiative called the Globe Project (House et al., 2004). The Globe Project was significant because it received participation of researchers worldwide. The Globe Project facilitated scholarly acceptance by garnering a wide level of international participation. Co-researchers collated data in over 62 countries and interviewed over 17,300 middle managers.

Globe Project Methodology

The approach to the Globe Project research was akin to a theoretical construct researchers used in the study of ALS. The ALS ultimately developed a mean for all of the direct reports. Researchers then attributed this mean to a leader's style of engagement with direct reports. It became a norm of leadership practices. The Globe Project expanded the number of personal traits Hofstede research utilized from six to nine (House et al., 2004).

The design of the research also consisted of
convenience sampling of 17,300 members of middle
management across 62 different countries by different
researchers. The researchers used a single survey.
The survey was available in the researchers'
respective languages, and interpreters translated the
completed responses back into English. The
investigators goal was to collect data from 300 local
managers from each of their geographic regions. The
survey had five sections. Each section dealt with a
specific question that inquired about the national
culture, participants' perceptions of 56 leadership
characteristics, and their perceptions of an ideal
society based upon 39 questions on a 7-point Likert-
type scale concerning value, leadership evaluation,
and demographics.

Significance and Limitations

The researchers of the Globe Project were
ambitious. The Globe Project had implications
throughout the field of leadership study. The Globe
Project brought attention to the potential impact
cultural differences might have on the dyadic

relationships of leader-members.

The research energized the discussion on the number and type of elements for consideration in data collection and analysis (House et al., 2004). Despite the data the Globe Project contributed to the leadership body of knowledge (House et al., 2004), there were limitations and weaknesses in its assessment that contributed to the questionable validity of leadership research. The research design was not rigorous, and it had areas of subjectivity and potential data corruption.

The challenges to the appeal and value of a study on the international scale was, first, the risk of using culturally diverse researchers to collect local data. Variations in researcher experience and objectivity increased the risk to the validity of data. Second, translation to and from foreign languages and cultures potentially created conflicts in identifying themes within the qualitative data.

The researchers' Average Leadership Style (ALS) approach to the Globe Project may have discounted variances that might have existed between individuals. Theoretically, a leader could have had a significantly positive relationship with some subordinates and significantly bad relationships with others, and still receive an ALS score similar to a leader with a moderate relationship with a single subordinate. This acknowledged shortcoming in this construct may have given credibility to the LMX construct that promoted inquiry into the leader-member dyads, resulting in encouraging more researchers to migrate to the LMX model.

Noteworthy Gap in Recent LMX Research

As a result of increased diversity within the workforce, there was an increase in the attention to the effect inclusion of minority employees has on the organization. The findings of the Globe Project (House et al., 2004) supported assertions there was value in gaining knowledge of the potential impact diversity had on the leader-member dyad. The literature review showed evidence of attention to quantitative assessments and those interactions that created a positive or high-quality LMX relationship. There was little attention to the low-quality LMX relationships that created an out-group of the supervisor's workforce.

This literature review of the development from VDL to LMX focused heavily on the paradigm and research approach shifts. From seminal research to today, the acknowledgment of identifying standard metrics and the focus on dyad strength marked the major stages of maturation. As in any theory, definition was the first and foremost responsibility of seminal researchers who desired to disseminate new research knowledge and conclusions.

For other researchers to build upon that new knowledge, there must be consistency within the metrics and level of analysis. Schriesheim et al. (1999) covered over 140 LMX studies in a comprehensive review of LMX research. Schriesheim et al. highlighted the dynamic nature of assessed sub-dimensions that may affect the dyad. The lack of consistency supports the assertion the research had been exploratory and had not built upon previous knowledge or added depth to knowledge in any specific aspect of LMX research. Rousseau (1998) steered the scholarly discussion from whether the LMX theory existed, and which factors affected the theory to its outcomes or effects. Rousseau referred to this lack of information on the outcome of LMX as a black-box descriptor of the emptiness and void.

The research community acknowledged this apparent gap in the knowledge in 2009, when researchers noted a lack of research on those subordinates-assigned, out-group statuses. Bolino and Turnley (2009) proposed a theoretical model to address this perceived gap in knowledge on out-groups, also known as low-quality dyads. Bolino and Turnley presented 12 propositions for further research the gap of knowledge in LMX low-quality dyads. Although the researchers discussed these propositions in correlation to another social theory, Bolino and Turnley highlighted the lack of attention on understanding the low-quality experience.

Qualitative data provides the ability to develop theories to why certain dyadic phenomena exist within the LMX construct. The limited research into low-quality exchange relationships highlighted out-group subordinates' negative perceptions of their jobs, advancement opportunities, and inclinations to leave their positions (Gerstner & Day, 1997; Graen & Uhl-Bien, 1995; Maslyn & Uhl-Bien, 2001; Vecchio, 1986). There were indications in the research findings that individuals within the low-quality exchanges wanted

improved relationships with their leaders and wanted
to contribute to the organization (Maslyn & Uhl-Bien,
2001). The propositions of Bolino and Turnley (2009)
indicated a recognized gap in knowledge and the
desire to inquire into low-quality relational
phenomena.

Research in the last eight years (2011-2019)
remained mostly quantitative in nature with limited
qualitative inquiry (Gwynne, 2014; Walker, 2011).
Qualitative researchers continued to modify the
elements they measured to assess the strength of the
leader-member dyad. A recent study by Gwynne
(2014) focused on members of an organization who
had low-quality relationships with their leaders.
Gwynne (2014) found individuals in the low-quality
leader-member dyads had negative perceptions of
organizational justice and commitment. Wu (2010)
found value in understanding the perceptions of those
in the out-group. Wu conducted a quantitative, two-
part study that first measured an attribute labeled
Growth Need Strength (GNS), which in turn measured
the individual's job fit in correlation to being in the out-
group. The second part of the study reconciled the
GNS with whether an out-group member felt strongly

enough to change his or her status from out-group to in-group. Some out-group members exhibited a strong desire for growth. Additional qualitative research on the out-group may yield information on the perspectives of out-group members and suggest ways to influence the need for growth. Both Wu(2010) and Gwynne (2014) suggested a need to explore the aspects of out-group members further to address the lack of knowledge of the other half of the LMX construct continuum.

Acknowledging that the predominant research in the LMX field is quantitative in nature or focuses on high-quality relationships, the gap in the research is the lack of qualitative studies of the low-quality dyads within LMX. There is a further shortage of qualitative literature exploring specific racial demographics that have low-quality leader-member dyads within the LMX theory construct. There is no indication that this knowledge gap will receive any large-scale focus due to the apparent desire of seminal LMX researchers to continue to explore and expand LMX rather than to add depth or validation to the knowledge already gained. For example, Graen and Schiemann (2013) turned their focus to leadership-motivated excellence theory (LMX-T) as an extension of LMX. Although Graen and Schiemann (2013) asserted the LMX-T research was a focused, postmodern LMX leadership approach that promoted understanding of the job fit difficulties of millennials, it supported the conclusions of this literature review.

CHAPTER 3
METHODOLOGY

Introduction

The purpose of this qualitative study was to understand the personal experiences of African-American subordinate employees in the out-group of the LMX dyadic relationship and to gain insight into how they viewed themselves and their working relationships. The researcher defined the diverse demographic as the ethnic difference between the manager and the employee. The researcher investigated the perspective of African-American subordinate employees in the LMX out-groups of Caucasian supervisors and identified factors that enhanced or detracted from the development of the professional relationship. The research question of this study was:

*How do African-American, subordinate
employees within the out-groups of their
Caucasian immediate supervisors, as
defined by the LMX theory, describe
their leader-member dyad narratives?*

Research Design

The research design was an exploratory,
qualitative inquiry that, after data saturation through
purposive data collection, reduced individual
participants' perspectives to the meanings they
ascribed to the experience. The researcher identified
common themes and presented them as research
findings (Androff, 2010). Purposive sampling was
necessary because a specific demographic was
critical in successfully gathering relevant data that
addressed the research question (Stebbins, 2001).

The researcher collected data until saturation
was achieved via recording and the use of word-
processing documents (Bernard & Ryan, 2010). The
researcher utilized NVivo 10, which imported data
from documents, and assisted with sorting, coding,

categorizing, and inductive analysis of each leader-
member dyad. This software assisted the researcher
in adhering to the research process and reduced
potential researcher bias. The researcher utilized a
qualitative inquiry design to document the experience
of African-American subordinate employees who were
members of the LMX out-group. This inquiry was a
means of researching the meanings individuals or
groups ascribed to social or human phenomena in
which these individuals or groups participated
(Androff, 2010). The research question that guided
this study inquired how African-American subordinate
employees within the out-groups of their Caucasian
immediate supervisors, as defined by the LMX theory,
described their leader-member dyad narratives. The
exploratory qualitative inquiry design provided the
best parameters and constructs in which the sample
population could provide data that was relevant to the
research question.

The researcher solicited participants for the
study utilizing a web and blog posting. Upon
notification of interest, the researcher sent an e-mail
to potential participants explaining the requirements
for completion of the LMX-7 Questionnaire and

Demographics Screening Instrument. The researcher used the LMX-7 Questionnaire developed by LMX seminal researchers Graen, Novak, and Sommercamp (1982) to identify members of the LMX out-group. The researcher requested and received permission to utilize the LMX-7 Questionnaire.

Upon review of the LMX-7 Questionnaire and Demographics Screening Instrument results, the researcher purposively selected a sample of the population to ensure maximum variance. The researcher asked the participants to complete an Informed Consent Form and confirm their self-identified race during the interview. The researcher interviewed those consenting to participate with the questions in Appendix A. A transcriptionist who signed a confidentiality agreement prepared a transcript of the interview(s). The researcher sent the transcripts back to the participants for validation with further instructions. Upon receipt of the validated transcripts from the participants, the researcher analyzed the data.

Sample Frame

The population of focus was self-identified,
ethnically African-American, subordinate employees
who were part of the LMX out-group of a Caucasian
(white ethnicity) immediate supervisor of a minimum
of one year. Ethnicity referred to a category of people
who identified with one another based upon a shared
ancestry, experience of culture, and social interaction.
The U.S. Census Bureau defines an African-American
(black) as a person of color with origins of African-
American ancestry via racial groups from Africa
(Humes et al., 2011; U.S. Census Bureau, 2013).

The sample frame consisted of self-identified,
ethnically African-American, subordinate individuals
who experienced low-quality LMX dyads with their
Caucasian immediate supervisors of at least one
year. All potential participants were English-speaking
adults who were 18 years or older. The researcher
screened participants for inclusion in the study with
the LMX-7 questionnaire and further identified
participants with the inclusion criteria (listed below).
The LMX-7 questionnaire determined subordinates'

perceptions of their LMX dyads. The researcher considered potential participants scoring within the range of 7-19 on the low end of the LMX-7 scale and classified them as members of the out-group. The researcher excluded potential participants who scored between 20 and 35, as the researcher considered them as part of the in-group, as measured by the LMX-7 scale.

The researcher utilized purposive sampling to select from the population those who ultimately provided the best interpretation and understanding of the experience of African-American subordinate employees within the LMX out-groups of their immediate Caucasian supervisors (Cooper & Schindler, 2008). The researcher utilized the participant scoring of the LMX-7 questionnaire in conjunction with the inclusion criteria in Table 1 to determine the sample.

Table 1 - Research Sample Inclusion and Exclusion Criteria

Criterion	Inclusion	Exclusion
Ethnicity	Self-identified African-American	Self-identified other than African-American
Age	18 and above	17 and younger
LMX-7 Score	7-19	20-35
Spoken Language	English speaking	Non-English speaking
Employment Supervisor	Ethnically Caucasian	Ethnically other than Caucasian
Supervisor/Subordinate Duration	One year or longer	Less than a year

The researcher used four recruiting techniques: (a) contracting the professional research recruitment services of SurveyMonkey, (b) as a secondary approach, utilizing a snowballing recruitment method at the conclusion of interviews of successfully recruited participants potentially to capitalize on early successful recruitments, (c) upon receiving site permission and IRB approval, soliciting professional and common interest groups (i.e. African-American Employees Online and African-American Employees Network) on the social media sites LinkedIn and Facebook. The researcher then posted the recruitment flyer as directed by the site moderator (i.e., discussion forum, classified section, blog, e-mail

or announcements), and (d) posting flyers on public
community bulletin boards. The researcher based the
selection of participants on the inclusion and
exclusion criteria in Table 2.

Table 2 - Demographics Screening Instrument

---

*Introduction: The purpose of this instrument is to
collect demographic data that enables the researcher to
ensure data collection occurs from a maximum variation of
sampled population. Circle appropriate selection.*

Age

18-30   31-40   41-50   51-above

Sex

Male   Female

Education Level (highest level completed)

High   Associate's   Bachelor's   Graduate
School   Degree   Degree   Degree
Diploma

Category of your present employment (select closest
relation):

☐ Government   ☐ Technology
☐ Manufacturing   ☐ Finance
☐ Education   ☐ Service

Length of management relationship (How long have you
worked for the current supervisor; circle one):

1-5 years   6-10 years   11-15 years   16+ years

The sample size sought for this exploratory
qualitative inquiry was a minimum of 15 and a
maximum of 20 participants designated as an out-
group using the LMX-7 scale (Robson, 2002). The

eventual sample was 17 participants. The concept of data saturation was collection of data until no new information emerges (Morse, 1995). Data saturation was also known as data adequacy. The qualitative research method characteristically utilized smaller samples due to the large amount of data that emerges during in-depth interviews (Crouch & McKenzie, 2006). The nature of this research and questions required in-depth interviews to elicit the desired data. The researcher chose the exploratory, qualitative inquiry research design as the most effective research method for this study. The purposive solicitation of individuals utilizing a social-media site reduced participant risk and mitigated potential researcher bias due to familiarity.

Instrumentation

The instruments utilized for this study were the researcher, the LMX-7 questionnaire, demographics screening, and the primary data collection instrument. These instruments supported the administration of an interview protocol outlined later in this chapter.

Prequalifying Data Collection and Demographics Screening Instruments

The researcher used the LMX 7 Questionnaire as the prequalifying test instrument to determine low-quality LMX dyads. The researcher obtained permission from the author to use this questionnaire for the study. The researcher gathered the demographics of potential participants by utilizing the demographics screening instrument.

Primary Data Collection Instrument

The researcher's initial communications with potential participants followed patterns established in the developed interview protocol. The researcher was the primary data collection instrument, conducted face-to-face, telephone, or online video conferencing interviews. These interviews consisted of 12 open-ended questions about the interviewees' descriptions of their experiences in an ethnically diverse supervisor-subordinate relationship. An expert panel for conceptual validity reviewed the interview questions. The interview questions are listed in Table 3.

Table 3 - Data Collection Instrument: Interview Questions

Question (Purpose)

1. Describe the organization with which you are currently employed. (Demographics; LMX)
   * Describe how your organization ensures diversity and inclusion of workforce. (Demographics; LMX)
   * Describe your responsibilities within your organization. (LMX)
2. Describe how your supervisor assigns the tasks of your job.
3. How many of your peers/coworkers work for the same supervisor?
   * Describe the interactions you have with your immediate supervisor. (LMX)
4. Describe the interactions the supervisor has with all individuals subordinate to him or her.
   * Describe your supervisor's leadership style. (LMX)
5. What are the factors you believe influence the leadership style he or she uses with you?
6. (if coworkers) How does he or she apply his or her leadership style to all?
   * Describe the reward and discipline system within your organization. (LMX)
7. What process is in place to ensure equity in the application of the awards and discipline process?
   * Describe how you feel you make contributions to this organization. (LMX)
8. How does the organization recognize you and others for those contributions to the achievement of the objectives of the organization? (LMX)
   * What do you feel is your responsibility for the relationship that has developed between you and your supervisor? (LMX)
9. What organization procedures or processes are in place that control or shape the relationship you have with your supervisor? (LMX)

Question (Purpose)

10. How do you cope with the current situation in your job?
(LMX)
11. What would you do differently if you had an opportunity
to reestablish your relationship with your supervisor?
(LMX)
12. How would you describe the impact the relationship
with your supervisor has on your productivity, job
satisfaction, and motivation? (Closeout Question: LMX)

* Denotes probing questions

Role of the Researcher

In this exploratory, qualitative inquiry, the
researcher served as the instrument of data collection
within the framework of this model (Lincoln & Guba,
1985. The researcher collected the data during
interviews conducted with the sample population
(Moustakas, 1994). The researcher served as the
analyst of the data. The researcher utilized epoche to
manage potential bias. In this step, the researcher
remained cognizant of and noted the potential impact
of his bias, preconceptions, and beliefs about the
experience. The researcher set aside his personal
experiences and bias at the following periods utilizing
prescribed methods to ensure the researcher gave
adequate focus to epoche:

1. The researcher annotated experiences and biases before initiating data collection. This step mitigated the impact of researcher bias and prepared the researcher to view the data and meanings on their merit.

2. The researcher solicited the research participants purposively from a social media site and thereby reduced the possibility the researcher would be familiar with the participants or the organizations for which they worked.

3. Upon completion of data collection, the researcher again reviewed previously annotated personal perspective and bias to ensure the researcher did not induct personal bias into the analysis process.

Background and training. The researcher was the primary instrument for data collection. The researcher was a senior officer in the U.S. Marine Corps. The researcher's over 21 years of experience as a Marine Corps officer enhanced communication skills. While the researcher served as a commissioned officer, the researcher often had to conduct command investigations. These

investigations were qualitative in nature and often
resulted in extensive face-to-face interviews and
phone interviews, note taking, transcripts, and
development of themes that resulted in findings and
recommendations. This investigative process was
parallel to the qualitative research method. The
researcher's experience in exploratory, qualitative
inquiry also included the completion of the following
Capella University courses: Survey of Applied
Research Methods and Advanced Qualitative
Research Methods. These courses refined the
researcher's understanding of the qualitative research
process. The researcher's three years as a college
instructor also assisted in strengthening written and
verbal communication skills.

New experience. While the researcher was
experienced with the interview process, the
researcher enhanced those skills with additional
specific experience. To ensure interview skills were
fully honed, the researcher conducted field-testing of
the interview questions before conducting the
interviews. The researcher utilized NVivo 10
qualitative research software to assist in data

analysis. The researcher did not have experience in using the software. However, a company named QSR, which produced the NVivo software, offered online training: workshops to train individuals on use of the software and the intricacies of coding. There were also tutorials available on YouTube. The researcher conducted online training before beginning of the analysis.

Data Collection

The data collection method was via telephone interview. This method was pertinent to the research question because it allowed the researcher to elaborate on questions as required. The research questions focused on eliciting personal information. The data-collection method also allowed the researcher to note inflections in voice and tone when responding to questions that the researcher might not otherwise have noted. The researcher formatted each question to provide insight into each construct. Data collection procedures included the following:

Preparatory Phase. The researcher coordinated a time to conduct interviews via telephone. The researcher ensured recording capability was available using the conference call service. To facilitate a comfortable telephone interview, the researcher utilized a conference call system, which allowed the participant to call from the phone of his or her choice and a time of his or her choice.

Initial Phase. The researcher welcomed the participants, briefed them on the purpose of the study, and requested informed consent. The researcher reminded participants that the researcher would record the interviews and answered any questions the participants asked.

Interview Phase. The researcher asked the interview questions. The researcher ensured the participants understood the questions and utilized probing questions as necessary. the researcher obtained the respondents' contact information: phone number, address, and e-mail address for a later review of the transcript.

Closing Interview Phase. The researcher asked the final interview question to ensure all the data the participant wished to share on the topic was captured. After the participant had completed the last question, the researcher informed the participant the interview was over. The researcher reminded the participant of the requirement to review the transcript of the interview and any follow-up questions as needed. The researcher reminded the participants they would receive a $50 gift card for participation after the participant transcript review. The researcher sent guidance to facilitate member-checking along with a copy of the transcript for member-checking.

Data Analysis

The researcher utilized thematic analysis to search across the data set of interviews to guide the identification of patterns within the text of the narratives of the participants (Braun & Clark, 2006). The three primary types of thematic analysis were inductive, theoretical, and thematic with a constant comparison. The researcher utilized the inductive type of thematic analysis for this study. According to Taylor and Bogdan (1998), the process of thematic analysis is not simple. In the inductive form of analysis, the researcher remained objective and did not attempt to guide the analysis based upon his previously conceived notions in regard to the subject. The researcher set aside pre-existing understandings. The researcher analyzed the data collected from the participants individually. Upon completion of the analysis of all participant data, the researcher synthesized the repeated patterns and themes to extrapolate a coherent theme for the data. The inductive analysis process followed with the steps listed below:

1. The researcher reviewed the data collected from each participant (interviews).
2. The researcher read the transcripts and intuitively highlighted any phrases with potential meaning or significance.
3. The researcher reconciled the highlighted data to ensure alignment with the research question.
4. The researcher coded each data segment to track the individual items of data.
5. The researcher formed clusters of relatable data

to form patterns, which were then coded. The researcher developed a second level of code if the data were rich enough to support developing subsets of patterns.

6. The researcher utilized the patterns identified to search for a common theme.

7. Upon completion of the data analysis, the researcher aligned the themes in a matrix commensurate with the patterns previously identified. The matrix included codes to assist in interpretation of data and presentation of the final report.

8. The researcher provided a narrative describing the relevance of themes and their respective patterns and codes.

9. The researcher assessed the narrative provided by each participant as part of this process.

10. The researcher consolidated all assessments.

11. Finally, the researcher sanitized the data and synthesized the themes to develop overall findings

The researcher utilized NVivo 10, which imported data from Word documents and assisted

with the sorting, coding, categorizing, and analysis of
each leader-member dyad. This software assisted the
researcher in maintaining the discipline of the
research process and reduced potential researcher
bias.

Validity and Reliability

The use of data collection instruments others
had developed and proven through psychometric
discipline and field tests facilitated the validity and the
reliability of the study. Graen and Uhl-Bien (1995)
developed the LMX-7 Questionnaire the researcher
utilized for this study. The use of the LMX-7
Questionnaire facilitated the researcher's ability to
reconcile theoretical constructs of this study with
previous research.

The validity of the data collection instrument
was supported by field tests of interview questions.
Two non-study participants who shared the same
characteristics of the study population conducted the
field tests. The field-test of the interview protocol and
questions aided in ensuring participants understood
the questions, fostered proper responses, and

facilitated the generation of relevant data within the allotted hour time-frame. Two field-test participants completed the questions within the allotted time. The researcher neither collected nor retained data during the field test.

To ensure the validity of the interview questions, the researcher made modifications as a result of the two field-tests. The changes made to the inquiry and data collection instrument by the researcher were:

- Modification of leading interview questions that assumed a state or condition of the participant within the inquiry.
- Modification of interview question to ensure the questions reflected the qualitative, open-ended form and were not quantitative.
- Addition of probing questions to ensure the researcher gathered a full and rich response.
- Specification that participant response should focus on the current and not any past supervisor.

The field test also ensured the researcher was familiar with the interview protocol and epoche, which was the reduction of biases and preconceptions. The field test increased the researcher's potential for apprehending the structure of the experience as it appeared in the consciousness of the participant.

The researcher received coaching from the dissertation mentor regarding the development of interview questions to ensure alignment with constructs and the research question. The mentor reviewed the transcription of the interviews and provided feedback. The researcher adjusted the interview questions per feedback to align the interview questions better with the constructs and research question.

An expert panel of three individuals reviewed the interview questions for validity and relevance. All three individuals had experience in either diversity or qualitative doctoral research. Two expert panel members were from the U.S. Marine Corps Diversity Section, and managed the diversity and inclusion efforts for the Marine Corps. Each of the Diversity Branch individuals had over 20 years of experience in management and offered training at the Defense Equal Opportunity Management Institute in diversity management skills. The third expert was an

experienced qualitative doctoral independent
researcher.

Consent and Confidentiality Forms

All participants, to ensure they were informed
and agreeable to the study, provided a signed consent
form before participation. The details of the purpose
of the study and the outline of the protocol to protect
their confidentiality were noted in the consent form.

To facilitate the protection of the personal data
collected during this inquiry, the researcher ensured
the transcriptionist utilized was discreet and adhered
to the inquiry protocol for protection of participant
information. The transcriptionist completed a
confidentiality form. The participants reviewed their
transcripts for accuracy, which included the possibility
of additional and changed data.

Ethical Considerations

The researcher gave ethical consideration in
regard to respect for participants, beneficence, and
justice for the study participants. The study required

subordinates of an organization to discuss their perceptions of their supervisors. The researcher solicited the population from across international social-media sites and used a snowballing method, thereby limiting the potential for researcher conflict of interest or undue familiarity with the situations participants described. In case there was any emotional difficulty in discussing any situation, the researcher advised the participant that participation was optional and anonymous. The researcher ensured participation was voluntary and participants were not under any influence to complete the interview in any manner. To mitigate the potential for bias during the interview process, the researcher reviewed and completed training via collaborative Institutional Review Board (IRB) training initiative courses required for this type of study. The researcher followed ethical considerations the IRB required.

The researcher reviewed and designed the research approach giving consideration to beneficence, respect for persons, and justice, which are basic ethical principles within the Belmont Report. The researcher considered each of these areas of focus for relevance and took the appropriate mitigating actions to ensure the conduct of the study was in accordance with these ethical principles.

Beneficence

The researcher acted with beneficence toward the participants and ensured the findings were shared with those participating. The general rules of beneficent action the researcher adhered to were (a) do no harm and (b) maximize all possible benefits while minimizing possible harm (U.S Department of Health and Human Services, 1979). The researcher sanitized the data and findings so that no harm came to those who participated. The researcher shared the findings of the study to allow all participants to share in the potential benefits.

Respect for Persons

Respect for the participants was a primary planning factor in the design of the study. The ethical consideration of respect fell into two requirements: the acknowledgment of autonomy and the protection of those with compromised autonomy (U.S Department of Health and Human Services, 1979). The researcher ensured those participating did so voluntarily and were not under any pressure.

Justice

The researcher factored this ethical consideration into the design of the study to ensure five outcomes: first, to ensure equal shares to participants; second, to consider the need of the individual; third, to ensure the researcher considered the effort of the individual; fourth, to factor in the participant's contribution to society; and fifth, to consider the individual's merit (U.S Department of Health and Human Services, 1979). The researcher designed the research to ensure participants voluntarily participated at an equitable level. The researcher offered comparable compensation to all participants. The researcher paid the participants $25 per hour, with a maximum of $50 paid to each.

Conclusion

The researcher employed an exploratory, qualitative inquiry research design for this study. Purposive sampling was necessary because a specific demographic was critical in successfully gathering relevant data that addressed the research question (Stebbins, 2001). The researcher utilized epoche, bracketing, and member checking to facilitate and bolster the validity and reliability of the study.

A detailed report of the analysis of this study follows in Chapter 4. The analysis provided a venue to assess and document the experience of the African-American subordinate employee who was a member of the LMX out-group. The exploratory, qualitative-inquiry method was a means for researching the meanings individuals or groups ascribed concerning a social or human phenomenon in which these individuals or groups participated (Androff, 2010).

CHAPTER 4

RESULTS

Introduction

The purpose of this exploratory, qualitative
inquiry was to gain a greater understanding of the
personal experiences of African-American
subordinate employees in the out-group of the LMX
dyadic relationship and to gain insight into how they
view themselves and their working relationships. The
researcher defined a diverse demographic as an
ethnic difference between the manager and the
employee. The researcher investigated the
perspective of African-American subordinate
employees in the LMX out-groups of Caucasian
supervisors and identified factors that enhanced or
detracted from the development of the professional
relationships.

Research participants provided their personal
experiences as African-American subordinates of

Caucasian supervisors. The analysis included utilizing in-depth personal interviews as a unit of analysis; the research may foster a greater level of appreciation of the African-American experience based upon analysis of their narratives.

Sample Frame

The sample frame consisted of self-identified ethnically African-American subordinate individuals currently experiencing low-quality LMX dyads with their Caucasian immediate supervisors of at least one year. All participants were English-speaking adults who were 18 years or older. The researcher screened the participants for inclusion in the study with the LMX-7 questionnaire and further identified them with the inclusion criteria listed below. The LMX-7 questionnaire determined subordinates' perceptions of their LMX dyads. The researcher considered potential participants scoring within the range of 7-19 on the low end of the LMX-7 scale and classified them as the out-group. The researcher excluded potential participants scoring between 20-35 from the study, as the researcher considered them within the in-group by the LMX 7scale.

Inclusion Criteria

- Self-identified, ethnically African-American (persons of color)
- Age 18 and above
- LMX-7 Questionnaire score of 7-19
- English Speaking
- Employed with an immediate Caucasian Supervisor in a work relationship of a year or more.

Exclusion Criteria

- Self-identified ethnically other than African-American
- Age 17 or less
- Non-English speaking
- LMX-7 Questionnaire score of 20-35
- Employed with immediate supervisor not ethnically Caucasian or in a work relationship of less than a year
- Not-employed

Methodological Approach

The research method was qualitative. The
design was a qualitative inquiry that, after data
saturation through purposive data collection, reduced
the individual participants' perspectives to meanings
they ascribed to the experience whereby the
researcher could identify common themes and
present them as research findings (Androff, 2010).
Purposive sampling was necessary because a
specific demographic was critical in successfully
gathering relevant data that addressed the research
question (Stebbins, 2001).

The researcher collected data via
spreadsheets and word-processing documents until
data saturation occurred (Bernard & Ryan, 2010). The
researcher utilized NVivo 10, which imported data and
assisted with sorting, coding, categorizing, and
inductive analysis of each leader-member dyad. The
researcher utilized this software to facilitate the
research process and to reduce potential researcher
bias.

The researcher utilized thematic analysis to search the data set of interviews to guide the identification of patterns within the text of narratives of the participants (Braun & Clark, 2006). The three primary types of thematic analysis were inductive, theoretical, and thematic. The researcher utilized inductive analysis for this study. According to Taylor and Bogdan (1998), the process of thematic analysis was not simple. In the inductive form of analysis, the researcher remained objective and the researcher did not attempt to guide the analysis based upon his previously conceived notions on the subject. The researcher set aside preexisting understandings. The researcher analyzed the data the researcher collected from the participants individually. Upon completion of the analysis of participant data, the researcher synthesized the repeating patterns and themes to develop coherent themes.

Overview of Themes

Data analysis yielded 12 common themes through reconciliation of research participants' statements. The themes related to LMX theory were

rife with negative assertions of encounters,
environments, and manners by which the participants
coped and thereby affected the organization. The
specific themes and the number of coded references
to those respective themes are in Table 4, which
reflected the 12 themes with the most significant
representation in the sample population.. A detailed
explanation of these themes follows within the data
and results sections.

Table 4 - Thematic Coded Reference Overview

Theme	Number of Coded References
Negative supervisor interaction	105
Negative environment	103
Favoritism	46
Limited leader communication	42
Negative personal emotional impact	42
Perceived communication criticality	37
Lack of appreciation of skills	36
Inconsistent policy application	34
Leadership style: Laissez-faire	25
Leadership style: Authoritative	20
Leadership style: Micromanagement	11
Coping mechanism: Internal and external	23

Data Presentation

The researcher utilized the by-participant method for presentation of data. The by-participant method organizes and reports the various data from each participant separately. The researcher then synthesized the data, and this resulted in a consolidated matrix of themes, codes, and patterns. The final presentation of data included general themes from quoted portions of the narratives. The researcher reported the general themes or patterns of meaning found in the transcripts. The researcher did not append the transcripts in their entirety to the dissertation, but rather the researcher included a matrix of themes and a number of coded references. Collections of themes and meanings that were not in alignment with the research were eliminated.

Negative Supervisor Interaction

Since the sample came from the out-groups of the supervisors, the majority of the participants expressed a theme of negative-supervisor interaction.

These were situations that participants described as emotionally or physically stressful. The negative integration could also act as negative communication. It is likely that perceiving oneself as within the supervisor's out-group will lead to negative interactions with the supervisor. These negative interactions were likely on the lower level of the LMX paradigm, resulting in lower-quality relationships. The participants shared the following statements referencing this theme:

Participant 2

> [It] depends on the day. Usually, I try to get her buy-in that I know what I'm doing. If I have a question, I do ask. I do make sure that I am going forward following our mission statement, following the guidelines set for us by our company. But, a lot of times, I am shot down, and shot down in [a] public form [forum], so that diminishes my authority with my team.

Participant 2

I am not comfortable with it. If I do not
have my team's support ... if they see
that my direct supervisor is contradicting
me, then why should they listen to me?

Participant 2

Somewhat – not always professional.
Uses foul language. Will talk about
other subordinates in front of teams,
mention them by name and their
shortcomings. Talks about other
supervisors in front of the team,
mentioning shortcomings. So, not
professional whatsoever.

Participant 4

No. They were not. For instance,
assignments would be getting out, he
would come by and bring the

assignments to each desk, and tell
them, "Here's your assignment." But,
when he would get to my desk, he
would say, "Read this. Do you
understand?"

Participant 8

The interactions (laughs) were usually
… what's the word I'm looking for …
they were stressful interactions.

Participant 8

Uncomfortable.

Participant 8

It – not necessarily arguments or
confrontations. It was just very … it was
uncomfortable because she was hard to
read, and she did not, in the work
environment, have a lot of personality.

Participant 12

We are very, very different. And I think she realized very early on that I am at least as smart, if not smarter, than she is. Something that happened before I was hired that I thought was rather unusual: most of my other peers had two people that served as references, and they did their reference check. They checked about five or six people – everyone off my reference list – and co-references that I did not list. I almost felt like they cast a wide net across the university, throwing my name out there, "Do you know this person? What do you think about them?" So, that was a struggle. But, she also just began to treat me very differently during that second year, and that has kind of continued. Caused me a lot of stress. She was very – she creates cliques on her team. So, you are either in her clique or you are not. And I never was, regardless of how many times I tried to not necessarily change, but kind of accommodate what I thought she wanted. But, it just, you know, never happened that way. She would keep information from me or make decisions consulting other members of the team without consulting me, and a lot of other stories, but there was a real transition after my first year, in terms of how she treated me. And, that kind of continues to this day.

Participant 9

Yes. The interaction is, and has been since day one, distant. Different. Even when there is just that person and [me], there is like a wall there. Which, I obviously will point a finger and look at myself first deep within. I mean, I just do not get it. It seems as though, I mean, as I said, this individual's writing my evaluation, and they still do not know anything about me. I am not saying, "Hey, you know what, they should be giving me high-level evaluation just because," but I mean, my record speaks for itself, and my performance speaks for itself up to this point. And you cannot say, "Okay, you did not complete this task, you didn't complete this mission, you didn't do this or that." Nothing like that has been said or shown. But yet, I get graded, I feel, in a mediocre manner, just because. It is an heir apparent, when I have to say, "Excuse me sir, do you know what my job is? This is what I am trained in. You do realize that?" And it is kind of like, "Oh. Oh yeah, I know what you're trained in." But yet, it still continues, you know? And that's where I have an issue. Blatant disregard, just because.

Negative Environment

The environment of the participants may facilitate the interaction between the supervisor and employee. Participants made comments during the interviews implying the environment generated stressful conditions or promoted a particular type of action by individuals within the organization. The participants' statements suggested that – not only were the interactions with their leadership not positive – but also the experience within the environment of the relationship was negative. The participants shared the following statements references on this theme:

Participant 5

I believe it was the [cultural] upbringing in the [geographic] area. It is a predominantly Caucasian county, and it is very racist in that area. You see all types of names in graffiti all of the place, it is very, very (laughs) pro-Caucasian.

So, I believe it was more so her trying to figure out … and when I say pro-Caucasian, that means nothing but Caucasian, I don't see any other shade of any other color. So, Hispanic, if you were of color, it doesn't matter – Hispanic, African-American, Chinese – just that environment made you feel like everything else is beneath Caucasian. So, I believe it was just her upbringing, and since it had been there since, obviously, a long time before I was born, it is kind of hard to stray away, in that small county, that is all you know. So, now you are trying – if I were to put myself in her shoes, I mean, it is kind of hard, and you are almost – I want to say she is about maybe in her 50s, maybe 60s, and you have been taught that for 50, 60 years, that you are supreme, it is kind of hard to turn that switch off. You might feel as though it is wrong, but it is kind of hard to, I guess, not be that way.

Participant 5

A lot of the times, it was dismissed,
because they felt as though I knew
more, and since this little African-
American girl does know more, she
knows the rules for these individuals
who have these disabilities, I was a
threat. So, a lot of the times, the
teacher's responsible – I would be told,
"The teacher is responsible for handling
her classroom or his classroom." So, it
would be … it got to the point where, if a
teacher wanted my assistance, I would
assist them. If a teacher did not want
my assistance, I would not assist them
(laughs). So … (laughs).

Participant 8

No, as an organization. That was
something you kind of had to figure out.
There were not a lot of leadership, how-

to-lead-and-manage type programs put
in place so that managers understood
how to balance their direct reports and
how to balance giving feedback and
how to balance coaching, how to give
constructive criticism, how to give
praise. There was not a lot of guidance
for managers on how to do that within
the organization.

Participant 12

We actually have coordinators or
directors of diversity inclusion in each of
the 10 colleges at our university. How
those positions operate is a little bit
different from college-to-college. Some
operate as far as being a liaison to
students to ensure that students are
involved. The way our coordinator
worked, she played that role, advised
student organizations as well as
coordinating the diversity part of our
first-year orientation course. In other

colleges, the person will do that in
addition to serving as a faculty liaison
and a college representation on different
diversity subcommittees. So, in some
places, it is one role, and in other places
it is two roles, and different colleges
have different resources that they place
towards trying to achieve diversity and
inclusion for students. Unfortunately,
there is very little to none, to my
knowledge, that is ever employed in
terms of educating faculty or staff as a
requirement. There are a lot of options,
but unless you are encouraged and
allowed by your supervisor, sometimes it
can be a struggle, depending on what
your role is.

Participant 12

Well, I feel theoretically good. But when
I look at how things have gone in
practice, particularly in the last year, I
am troubled, as I am an academic

advisor, I have a caseload of about 500 students of my own, and I teach a course on diversity to off-campus transfer students. I can tell you that many of our students of color do not feel supported. And so, that is a struggle for me.

Participant 13

There was someone in place, a person of color, female, in place, for, I would say, our department. But, the person did not feel that they were getting the support that they needed to develop the programs for the students, as well as faculty and staff, so they left and went to another department where they felt more comfortable in being able to really do the outreach that they felt that they could not do here. I will try not to say too much....

Participant 25

I felt that it was a noble, noteworthy cause, to at least acknowledge that you do need some diversity, because America is a diverse country. And the leadership, or, people who are in charge of America, are not really diverse. But, I applaud them for taking that effort, to at least recognize and try to organize some sort of effort to bring forth attention to that area of diversity, that we need to be more mindful of. So yeah. But, I felt like it was a feeble attempt, though. I mean, it was not well-received by the different organizations, because everyone was expecting their month, or their time to shine. It was not well-received by the people who they were trying to recognize.

Favoritism

A major observation of the participants was the
favoritism exhibited by the supervisor. The researcher
defined favoritism as those within the LMX high-
quality relationships receiving more benefits than
those in the lower quality relationships. The
participants shared the following statements
referencing this theme:

Participant 2

> Not necessarily, she has what I would
> deem an unprofessional relationship
> with some of the teammates, where ...
> setting some of them up on dates, going
> out with some of the other ones, and
> drinking.

Participant 3

> My position, I am an African American
> female, and my position was equivalent

to that of a Caucasian male. However, I
was not at – early on, I knew it was too
much work for one person to roll out a
system in six months, to make it fully
functioning, and [I] asked for an
additional resource, but [I] was not given
one. But, my Caucasian counterpart
was.

Participant 7

Well, to me, it seems like there is a
show of favoritism to other employees.

Participant 7

That is just how I feel because there
have been certain instances where
someone may, you know, for example,
for this particular woman to be able to
makes those type of comments to me
and not be reprimanded. Now, I have
never tried that, because I am a
professional and that is just not how I

conduct myself at work. But, at the same time, if I were to say something like that, I am sure it would be, you know, the consequences would be much, I think they would be much different for me. And, the reason I say that there is favoritism, because there are certain employees that, we have a certain amount of vacation time and off time, and sometimes we get to work from home, and then they will say, "Oh, you cannot work from home," but then this other employee who has been there longer is able to work from home.

Participant 12

Favoritism, is that a leadership (laughs) style?

Participant 12

I mean, she really – even the Dean of our college knows who her favorite is. Pretty much everyone across the

campus knows who her favorite is. And,
it is really odd, because she starts out
being very supportive, and then after
that first year, she seems to change.
She has a fair number – she comes
across as very confident, but internally,
she is very insecure. So, that really
comes out in her supervisory style. She
does not like to be shown as wrong; she
does not like to be shown up. She likes
to be the expert all the time, to the point
where she rarely, if ever, will take on a
task that is new or unique, because she
has to be the expert in all things. And
she is very analytical, she is very
strategic, but she is also very
manipulative, and she has manipulated
people on the team so that she always
comes out to be kind of the golden girl.
And it took folks, when I was suffering
through this in my second year, nobody
really wanted to see it. But, as she
started trying to turn other people in the
office against each other, including the

other African-American professional
female that was in the office, it became
evident how manipulative she really
was.

Participant 14

You could see blatant favoritism in the
office. In order to get certain things you
wanted done, you had to go to someone
else for them to go to her, so it looks like
it is their idea, so that she will approve it.
So, you learned early on how to work
the system (laughs) pretty much, if you
wanted to get stuff done. It was not a,
"This is the policy, this is what we are
going to do, this is how we manage the
office for everyone." It is, "I like her, so
whatever she says, cool beans, let's do
that. And, yeah, you do not really matter
so much, so yeah, whatever you are
saying, even if it is fantastic, we are not
doing that." So, leadership, she bred an
office of division, pretty much.

Participant 15

Well, I am not recognized (laughs) for
the contributions I make in the current
department, which is really mind-
blowing to me, because I have been, the
earlier years at the University, in each
department I have been in. But, this
department, I just feel like the manager,
for some reason, is … I do not know, he
recognizes everyone else for anything,
(laughs) but I am not getting recognition
that is due.

Participant 9

In my opinion, totally different. From a
casual good morning, to a work
exchange, it is just a difference that I
can see myself, not only I can see, but
other people around me can see it. But,
it is kind of one of those things where if
it is not really affecting them, they are

like, "Oh, you know, man, I really feel
bad for you, but it is not affecting me,"
so they could care less. So, I mean, I
wonder, a lot of it seems, I do not know
if it is personality-driven or what. And, I
have asked, "Hey, is there an issue? Is
there a problem?" And I have gotten,
"No, no, everything is fine." But, yet it
continues.

Limited Leader Communication

There was a common theme among the
participants that their supervisors exhibited limited
communication. Participants desired greater
communication of (work) expectations. However,
participants routinely stated that interaction with their
supervisor was sparse, electronic, and rarely in depth.
The participants shared the following statements
referencing this theme:

Participant 1

Interaction … more weekly, because I
was pretty much left to my own devices.
Of course, I was given SOA [?? 5:59],
and [?? 6:01] indicated [?? 6:01]. But, as
far as the day operational tasks,
projects, that was more weekly, as far as
getting updates. Sometimes bi-weekly,
depending upon the projects, or if we
had staff meetings. So, e-mails, phone
calls.

Participant 5

I really did not have a lot of direct
interaction with the principal. We had a
lot of interaction with the assistant
principal. We saw the assistant principal
more often than we saw the principal.

Participant 5

Wave (laughs). A wave, or, "You are
talking too loud outside of the hallway."
We would get things like that, as if my
interaction with her was as if I were just
another student. That is how I felt with
my principal, my overall supervisor.
Yeah, that is how a lot of us felt, but me
personally, since you are thinking of me,
(laughs), that is definitely how I felt. It
was always something nitpicky. She
would talk – and the way that she talked
to you, it was as if she was talking to a
student, and I did not like that either.

Participant 5

Her leadership style was very, I would
say, passive-aggressive. She would not
directly sometimes – there was
something that she wanted you to do,
but versus just telling you what it is, she

would smile, let you walk by, let you go
to your classroom, and then either send
you an e-mail – now, she would also do
this with the teachers, unfortunately
(laughs). So, versus just telling me what
she needed before I walked all the way
to the classroom, she would send you
an e-mail. Versus – yeah (laughs).

Participant 7

Very removed. It is like he has … to be
quite honest, I feel like he has no
management skills. The only reason
that he is in the position he is in, is
because it is a family-owned business
and his father, pretty much, he retired,
and his son stepped in. But he [the son]
does not have management or
leadership skills.

Participant 8

> I ultimately believe … my strong personality and strong knowledge of the job that I was doing made it challenging for her to communicate with me.

Participant 9

> Yes. The interaction is, and has been since day one, distant. Different. Even when there is just that person and [me], there is like a wall there. Which, I obviously will point a finger and look at myself first deep within. I mean, I just do not get it. It seems as though, I mean, as I said, this individual's writing my evaluation, and they still do not know anything about me. I am not saying, "Hey, you know what, they should be giving me high-level evaluation just because," but I mean, my record speaks for itself, and my performance speaks

for itself up to this point. And, you
cannot say, "Okay, you did not complete
this task, you did not complete this
mission, you did not do this or that."
Nothing like that has been said or
shown. But yet, I get graded, I feel, in a
mediocre manner, just because. It is an
heir apparent, when I have to say,
"Excuse me sir, do you know what my
job is? This is what I am trained in. You
do realize that?" And, it is kind of like,
"Oh. Oh yeah, I know what you are
trained in." But, yet, it still continues,
you know? And, that is where I have an
issue. Blatant disregard, just because.

Participant 25

It was more of an e-mail conversation,
more than a personal interaction. And, it
was either him providing guidance via e-
mail, or whatnot, or, if I had an idea that
I wanted to implement within my
organization, I would have to personally

go down to his office to see him and talk
to him, because I would like to have that
face-to-face-time to let him see me.
Then, after that, if we had to implement
something in writing, of course, if it had
to be signed, we would do that. But, my
interaction with him was mainly e-mail,
on a day-to-day basis.

Negative Personal Emotional Impact

Many participants felt their relationships had a
negative impact on them. The interactions elicited
negative emotional feelings that facilitated their
perceptions of the leader-member dyad. The
participants shared the following statements
referencing this theme:

Participant 4

For a while, to begin with, I felt like I
could not do anything right, I must not
be that intelligent, because everything
that happened that was the slightest bit

wrong was said that it was my fault. So,
to begin with, that was very demeaning.
But after I, like I said, I talked to the
woman, the first woman that I finally got
to hold up in the company in HR, and
she reaffirmed that, "Just do your job,
you will be fine, everything – you are
fine." So, I don't know if they had other
complaints on him or what, but she just
kept telling me to just do the best I could
at my job. And, I would do that. Now, it
did bleed over when I went home. All of
the things, all of the frustration that I had
held in for the 8-10 hours that I was at
work, came out when I got home.

Participant 5

I was devastated. So, luckily, I built a lot
of rapport with some of my students'
parents, and anytime they saw
something wrong, I would just tell them,
"You did not hear it from me, but these
are the individuals that you can report

this to." So, I had to advocate in other avenues. So, I had to let my parents know that they had every right to go to the school, the school board, to NACY, and the Department of Public Instruction, because they cannot get fired for advocating on behalf of their children. So, that is how I was able to get around that. But overall, I am still really disappointed that is a rule. Teachers are black-balled. A lot of teachers have been black-balled for advocating on behalf of their students, and there is nothing – there is no way around it, or, it takes a really long time for you to be reinstated back into the public-school system. I was like, "It is wrong, but my hands are tied, there is nothing really that I can personally do, not by myself, to make that change."

Participant 13

Frustrated, disappointed. Frustrated,
because you are seeing that there is a
need, but it is like some people did not
see that the need was that important.
And, it was disappointing that this
person did not get the support that they
needed to really get these programs and
get more people hired in certain areas,
because, especially in higher ed, and
working at certain institutions, students
of color like to see someone who looks
like them, whether they are Native-
American, African-American, [Eastern]
Indian, Asian. Just, students of various
diversities, they like to be able to see
someone who looks like them and
relate[s] to them, and even with some of
the males, they like to see more males
in professional staff settings that they
can relate to and talk to about certain
things. Even things not always about

academics. And, that is something I try to tell people, that sometimes students have other needs other than, "This course that I am taking, or I am having difficulty with this faculty." Just, having someone that they can relate to, they can understand where they are coming from.

Perceived Communication as Critical

A common theme among participants was the perception of the criticality of communication to the quality of the relationship with their supervisor. Several participants expressed that a higher quality and or quantity of communication with their supervisors could possibly improve their relationships with their supervisors. The participants shared the following statements referencing this theme:

Participant 1

Oh, what I feel is that, the communication, everything, it is part of

my responsibility to help nurture that
relationship.

Participant 1

So, communication and everything is
two ways. I had to do my part and they
had to do their part.

Participant 5

I guess my responsibility should have
been to continue to effectively
communicate, because, when I look at
the employee supervisor roles, you
should be able to freely communicate
with your supervisor about any needs
and wants that you may have, any of
your concerns. Unfortunately, I did not
feel that same way, with this particular
supervisor. So, to develop that type of
relationship, it was hard, because you
never wanted to make her mad. It was
about feelings. So, you never wanted to

go to her and say something that may have been needed, you know, either for the kids or for yourself, and rub her the wrong way, and that she treats you differently, or you might not get what you want, (laughs) that day, (laughs). So, my responsibility, whether I did it or not, was to continue to effectively communicate with her, regardless of what she wanted to hear, when she wanted to hear it. Did not matter. I should have still effectively communicated with her. And, a lot of times, I did, which is why she did not like me, because I would verbally say something to her, and then put it in writing in an e-mail, because she liked to do that about things she didn't like to talk about anyways. So, (laughs) I would communicate with her via e-mail a lot of times, mainly just to document what I had spoken to her. Or, what I said. That way, nothing could be taken out of context.

Participant 5

I think I would actually go in and physically talk to her more. I would go to the office anytime I had a problem or concern. I would go to her and be like, "Did you know that this that and the third is taking place?! Who do I need to contact? Who do I need to report? Because that is just unacceptable!" I wish I would have done that more to let her know that, yes, I am very vocal, no, I do not care if I am terminated because you do not like the fact that I am vocal, but you need to know and the whole office needs to know that I am not here for you, that I actually am here to work on behalf of these students. I work for your students, because your students are the ones that need me. And, you need for your students to graduate and go on to the next level. You know? So, I wish I would have done that.

Lack of Appreciation of Skills

Some participants perceived their supervisors overlooked their abilities. Several expressed a frustration with limited use of skills in their work. Some participants expressed a desire to do more if a supervisor recognized training, credentials, and/or skills. The participants shared the following statements referencing this theme:

Participant 2

Because, initially, we had to get to know each other, and I let her know what I felt my role in this position was, was to make her look good, that is my ultimate job, to make her look good. And, yet she had to learn to trust me on certain things, to let her know that I am here, I would not allow you to make yourself look like a fool. And I am there to kind of talk her off the ledge. But, she gets herself on a ledge too many times. So, I

am not sure (laughs) if I can do that
much talking. She is very judgmental.
So, again, I am not sure if anything I do
would change the situation.

Participant 3

The only thing that I would like to say, I
love all the questions so far, but in that
relationship, and as you are working and
gathering all this information, a key
piece that I feel that we – as women or
even African-American women or
African-American males or anyone in
the industry – to some degree, we have
to learn to take ownership of our careers
a lot further in advance than not. We
have to not look to someone else to
point out that you are great at this
skillset, because we are so used to
getting the job done and the task done,
we forget to go back and look at the
skills that we have acquired, and then
align ourselves accordingly. We are

waiting for someone else to point that
out, or, either point us out to go
somewhere else. Well, we should be
doing that ourselves. And, I think that is
something that is not spoken about, and
not really taught. And, because of that,
we find that, that may contribute as to
why some African Americans may not
be in greater leadership roles, because
they are waiting for someone to point
that out, versus them recognizing that
they have the ability to do that
themselves.

Participant 6

No. No, like I said, I was [never? 14:28]
trained for this in my current position, at
my current employer, and no one else
there has had the training that I had.
The training I received was from a
previous employer. No one else in my
current state of employment has the
type of training.

Participant 13

> With my job responsibility, it is pretty
> much laid out. So, I already know what
> to do, when to do, that type thing. But,
> what I get frustrated about is when, at
> times, I feel overlooked and boxed in.
> There was an opportunity; there was
> faculty in our department who wanted
> me to be a co-advisor to one of the
> student groups. But my supervisor said
> no because they did not feel that …
> well, it was not so much they felt I was
> not qualified, but they did not want
> others who were not of color to feel
> intimidated. Or, it was like they are
> being more accommodating to others,
> and not letting me grow in my field.

Participant 13

> I feel that I go above and beyond my job
> duties. I do things even after 5:00. I

participate in a lot of programming and
events in the area. I also do a lot of work
outside in the community as well. When
I see something needs to be done, I just
go and do it, even though it may not be
in my job description, if I see something
needs to be done, I just do it. And, I
notice now, not that this is a problem,
but they want to make sure the person
who is responsible for a particular duty
is doing their responsibility. So, I was
asked on certain things not to, to stop
doing that. If that person happens to be
out, that is one thing. But, they wanted
to make sure that person is doing what
they were supposed to be doing. And
that is under this new leadership person,
because in the past, a lot of things were
getting done and someone else was
getting credit for it, but then later they
found out that I was the one that was
doing that job or that work or what have
you, took care of whatever needed to be
done for that particular project or what

have you. So, now, they want to make sure that whoever is assigned to a project or something that is under their job description or responsibilities, that person [assigned] is actually doing it, and not someone else doing it and they [are] still getting the credit for it.

Inconsistent Policy Application

The participants perceived several leaders applied the policies of their organizations inconsistently. Participants acknowledged instances in which an action a leader took was clearly different for another than it was for them. The participants shared the following statements referencing this theme:

Participant 2

I think some of us have to work 10 times as hard to get it. Now, the overall award, as I said, it is a great one, it is the company-wide, so that is awards that are handed out among each individual office, I think those are handed out to favorites, or, "Hey, we need to give this to someone, so let us just give it to this person." Not based on merit, but just based on convenience.

Participant 3

My position, I am an African American female, and my position was equivalent to that of a Caucasian male. However, I was not at – early on, I knew it was too much work for one person to roll out a system in six months, to make it fully functioning, and asked for an additional resource, but was not given one. But my Caucasian counterpart was.

Participant 8

Other than ... hm. Not really. Because, being that you were a manager that had some discretion, even if the person wasn't worthy of the performance increase, you could still give them one. And, that could be based on the fact that, maybe there were some extenuating circumstances as to why they had a difficult year, or maybe it's someone who was new to their role, but you know that that person, in the next couple years, is going to do a great job, and you just want to reward them to motivate them. So, some of that was really discretionary, and there could have been favoritism based on the relationship you had with your manager, because the discretionary did not have to be the same across the board. You could give me an extra $1,000, and then you could give your five other direct reports an extra $3,000.

Participant 12

Right. Her favorite, she nominated for two university and national awards,

before she nominated anybody else on
the team for anything.

Participant 25

For the most part, I would say yes.
There were some (??). But that is still
subjective, though, because if I did not
put you in for a reward that you might
have deserved, you did not even get
started through the process. But, if you
did get put in, yeah, there was some
equity within the process to ensure the
reward you received was equal across
the board. And, likewise with the
discipline. Some things, discipline wise,
there were some things totally out of (??
17:29), what you did; again, some things
they might want to bring up, and push
more so than really needed to be.

Participant 25

I felt that my efforts were not being recognized. And, I was being diminished in some way. Though other, I would say my other four peers that I had, who were not doing anything of that nature, and I just felt that, for some reason, the supervisor was diminishing my roles and responsibilities and the efforts I had made, and were bringing the individuals who hadn't done as much up to par or even exceeding my efforts. I was not quite happy with it, and I kind of let it be known that I think that some of my efforts were, like I said, value added to the organization. I was hoping I would have gotten something more than a, "Oh, that was a nice spreadsheet," and that was it.

Leadership Style: Laissez-Faire

The participants perceived the leadership
styles of several of the leaders had characteristics of
a laissez-faire leadership. Laissez-faire is a policy of
being hands-off and not interfering with the process.
Several of the participants described their supervisor
as either consciously offering little guidance and/or
subconsciously interacting and offering a limited
amount of leadership. Participants expressed their
perceptions as follows:

Participant 6

First of all, he is very non-
confrontational. Except with a few of us.
He ... some of our [INAUDIBLE]
employees do what they want to do,
[INAUDIBLE] in some cases, is not
coming into work. And, that is okay with
some of them, because he does not like
disciplining them. I can recall a couple
instances where I actually had a

doctor's note to be off of work, and he questioned that. Even with a doctor's note.

Participant 7

Very removed. It is like he has … to be quite honest, I feel like he has no management skills. The only reason that he is in the position he is in is because it is a family-owned business and his father, pretty much, he retired, and his son stepped in. But, he does not have management or leadership skills.

Participant 20

He is definitely not a micromanager. He is very lax. Very loose. With very little organization, and very little structure. And I think that sometimes, he understands that, and he tries to compensate by [INAUDIBLE], maybe

that is where that comes into play. But
yeah, I would probably say, very
unorganized and very unstructured. That
is probably one of the better ways to
describe his leadership style.

Leadership Style: Authoritative

Participant 3

I would say ... authoritative, but, with
that thin liner of saying things in a way
that you have to question if it was
authoritative or not, because it was kind
of like, nice on the surface, but very
distinct and authoritative, but ... you
could not challenge that person [??
15:56]. So, if they came up with a
suggestion, and you thought something
different, if you verbalized that, you
immediately knew that that wasn't [the]
route you should have [taken], because
of the repercussions.

Participant 3

Because of the body language, I
immediately knew that person went on
the defense by how their body changed
with the seat back and the laying, you
know, your finger on the side of your
face, you kind of lean to listen, like....
So, immediately, I knew I had offended
the person. And then, from that day
forward, everything changed. I was
later told that, "You are not supposed to
challenge this person."

Participant 9

From my opinion, leadership is usually
defined as democratic or authoritarian,
and basically, I think this individual
leaves it open to discussion up until the
point that you are not saying what they
want to hear (laughs), and then the
discussion is kind of over, and then it is

like, the table slap, "I know that you said
that, alright, but we are going to go this
way, and that is the way it is going to
be." Now, basically I feel like others
within the section have way more
leeway to provide input or response to a
task or messages or any job-related
things. I think they have far more
leeway and are given far more leeway
than I am.

Leadership Style: Micromanagement

Participant 21

He was a pain in the butt (laughs). I
mean, if you want me to just get down to
it (laughs). He was like a control freak
to the highest power. He would
introduce himself as Colonel So-and-So,
or Lieutenant Colonel So-and-So.
Forget the fact that he'd been out of
military of at least six or seven years.
That is how he would introduce himself

to people that he was meeting now that he had the job with the city. I don't know why he thought that would make a difference. Until finally, one of these guys who was about 6'6" or so, one of our … [INAUDIBLE] this little guy, this little Chief Operations Guy went too far, and he tells him he would meet him outside and [INAUDIBLE] a little bit, and told him to stop going to meetings and looking like an idiot going around telling everybody that he was Colonel So-and-He wasn't in the military and he didn't wear his uniform. And, that was the way it went. So, when the mayor heard it, he made him stop. Because, he never did it in front of the mayor, he only did it when he was trying to be over someone.

Participant 2

There was a situation not too long ago where, when we ordered our cash for the week. I stated what I ordered before

I even placed the order. Then, the day before the orders – and I explained why I did what I did. And, the manager said, "Fine, that sounds good." So, the day before the order is coming in, she is looking at the numbers and trying to figure out why we ordered what we did, and I explained to her again, and yet, it was met with, "Well, no, that shouldn't be happening now. It's too early in the year, that's not the situation at the time." And, I'm trying to explain to her, "I have been in this area a lot longer, you just moved here from a different state. I've been in the area for seven, eight years, and this is usually the trend." And instead of saying, "Oh yeah, we talked about it," it was, "No, that just doesn't make any sense. No. We're going to send all that back." And, not only was it said with a, I guess, snippy attitude, it was said in front of a direct report. And so, to maintain my professionalism, I said, "That's fine," and I left the area.

Participant 4

> No. They were not. For instance, assignments would be getting out, he would come by and bring the assignments to each desk, and tell them, "Here's your assignment." But when he would get to my desk, he would say, "Read this. Do you understand?"

Coping Mechanism

A number of research participants expressed their interactions with their supervisors caused stress and frustration in their lives as a result of the low-quality relationships they had with their supervisors. As a result of the stress and frustration the participants experienced, they routinely developed coping mechanisms to assist in mitigating the negative impact of the stress. The participants shared the following statements referencing this theme:

Participant 3

I drunk a lot of Mountain Dew, I walked,
I would go outside, I would take breaks,
and I would walk. And, at the end of the
day, my self-fulfillment always comes
from me thinking, "I do a great job,"
because I set my inner peace on my
standard, and I have experienced this
more than once, only because, I feel
when you are on that technical side, this
technical field, I feel like, is still a
predominantly Caucasian male field.
And the higher you go up on that
technical side, you experience that.

Participant 4

I just went in and did my job, tried to be
as polite as possible to everyone,
treating everyone as civil[ly] as possible,
and just basically staying to myself and
getting my job done. But, I would also

help anyone else that needed
assistance. I did not – because, by then,
I realized that I was working for an
organization, and not necessarily for
one individual.

Participant 6

After a while of not getting the results
that you look for, you kind of … I guess,
keep it simple, I just lowered my
expectations. I say to myself quite often
that if you do not expect a lot, you will
never get disappointed. I lowered my
expectations to the fact that I know that I
would not get assistance where other
employees do. Yeah, I have just
lowered my expectations.

Participant 8

The coping mechanism I used was, I
only had to meet with her once every
other week. So, I just did what I had to

do to get my job done, keep myself
going. It was a great place to be in
reference to my business partners and
the field folk. They were awesome to
work with. That kind of kept me going
and kept me motivated. And, with her, I
ultimately just had to deal with her every
other week. Nobody was ever calling
her to complain about what I was doing,
or, if they could not reach me or could
not find me. So, she left me alone,
ultimately, that is how I coped with it.
Just made sure nobody called her to
complain, and then I did not really have
to spend much time with her.

Participant 12

Well, that's kind of the change that
happened in my fourth year. I went
home over Christmas break and had a
conversation with my father. My dad
has a unique way of looking at things,
but also, there was the former Diversity

and Inclusion person was someone's
office who I was in quite often. We had
very shared experiences in this college.
She had a different supervisor, but we
had a lot of the same environmental and
supervisory issues. She was a huge
support to me. Last year, when I went
home for Christmas, I was talking to my
father about my situation here, and he
said, "You know what? You can only
change your actions. You cannot
change anyone else's." So, from that
time on, I literally came in here, and I
am an introvert by nature anyways. I
kept to myself, and I did my work and I
did not make a whole lot of small talk
with anybody. That was a struggle. I will
say, I will share, that after my colleagues
that I was very close to, left, my level of
anxiety went through the roof. I won't
say I had to, but I decided in the spirit of
self-care to begin seeking out personal
therapy, so I see a psychologist on a
weekly basis. When my anxiety issues

got so bad that I was literally feeling
anxiety from, I would say, Saturday
through Wednesday, she suggested
anti-anxiety, anti-depression medication.
The work issues have compounded
personal issues that have been there for
many years, but when you work 50 or
60 hours a week in an environment, that
is your primary environment. When you
are under that kind of stress, I just, I
could not take it. And my source of
support within my office had left. So it's
like, when something happens now, I do
not have a sounding board, I do not
have a wall I can bounce it off, I do not
have a venting space. That has become
very challenging. My decision to stay
here was based on the fact that I really
wanted my next move to be to a Ph.D.
program, but I am a jack of all trades,
and I have a very wide variety of
interests, so, really honing-in on what is
my passion – a singular passion was
troublesome for me. I am much more of

an interdisciplinary thinker. This year,
when I gave myself permission, I
realized my head space is so clouded
here that it's not unusual or strange that
I can't clear my head space enough to
make decisions about my life. Hence the
seeking therapy. I have made decisions
that this upcoming year, I am essentially
– even though the things I do external
to my job are very fulfilling to me, and
much more along the lines of what I
want to do, it does make my job
problematic – so I have kind of made a
tentative decision to cut all of that,
because I really need to cut this back to
a 40-hour-work-week so I can begin to
make some decisions. But, if another
opportunity comes along, I have given
myself permission to leave here, even if
it is not to a PhD program, if it is just to a
better environment. So, I have been
looking for other work, but I am also
very cautious, because I personally
prefer the devil I know to the devil I don't

know. So, the positions I have seen
come open here recently, after I do
some investigation, I feel I learn they
may not be any better for me. So I am
proceeding with caution and continuing
with as much personal self-care as I
can, until I am able to find and
environment that I feel like understands
me and is supportive of what I have to
offer.

Participant 13

Um … well, prayer (laughs). And,
looking at the big picture. Students,
'cause a lot of students, they may not
realize that all this time, they do keep
me encouraged, by just saying that they
are glad to see me. Even some of them
who have already graduated, before
they graduated, they said please do not
leave me, wait until I graduate. They
have seen themselves the, at times, the
obvious disparity between staff and

professional staff, as well as people of
color versus non-people-of-color, and
they have expressed it themselves in
the classrooms. So, they have an idea.
So, the ones that graduate, they will
check on me, see how I am doing. That
is what keeps me motivated to continue
to come. I look at the big picture,
because I know there is something
better lined up, I just need to step
forward and go ahead. Like my
Master's, as I stated earlier, I need to
finish it so I can move on to something
else. And so, that is what keeps me,
(laughs) that is how I am able to cope.
That is a good question, because I do
get that question a lot from people in
general, regardless of ethnicity, I get that
a lot, because like I said, a lot of people
see things and they probably hear
things, [how in the world? 44:14]
(laughs). So, yeah, [INAUDIBLE] the
three things.

Participant 21

Oh, how did I cope? I thought about …
(laughs). Well, I had to do certain things
in order just to make things where they
were. One, what I was doing was so
high-profile, not just in the city, but in the
state, and through the federal
government, that he was kind of limited
on how much he could do to me after
that, once I became a Justice
Department person. The other thing –
so, that kind of limited it some. The
other thing is that, he himself, after the
mayor got all over him about some of
the things he was doing, that is when I
found out, later on, that a lot of what he
wanted to do is switch to my previous
supervisor, [who] was an African-
American lady. The one I told you he
would have come up and down the
stairs. She was my supervisor when I
first came to the Planning Department,

before I went to work for the Justice
Department. So, he got her involved.
So, he would pass a lot of dirty work to
her. Like, for instance, I developed a
database, and it was for all the grants
and things I had planned to use for the
city and for the Police Department, I had
it all sorted out. This woman did not
know very much about computers, but
what she was doing is, she would go
into my office and get into my computer
and try to see what I was doing, and
then go back and report to him. So,
what she did not know, because
[INAUDIBLE] what she did know was,
when you want to go on a computer, it
shows the last data that somebody has
been in that computer. So, if I am in
Washington on the 3rd, and I come back
and see that on the 3rd, somebody went
into my computer, I am trying to figure
out why all my files are all scrambled,
and then I found out it was her, because
one of the other employees told me

about it. Now, that was difficult to cope
with. They had tried to tell me before,
but this was supposed to be a religious
woman, she and I had supposedly been
friends, I didn't realize – now, they had
warned me before how she could be,
about how jealous she was and things
she was saying. But I am thinking, "No,
she would not do that, I know this lady, I
have been helping her to do stuff, I've
helped her career." Then I found out
they were telling the truth. That was the
hurtful part, when you find out the
person – you are not only helping them,
but you are going out of your way to
help them, and keep this other person
from harming them, and then they end
up doing all this stuff to you. That was
the hardest emotional part of the whole.
The Chief Operations Officer, I knew he
hated women, I knew he hated African-
American people, I knew he was power
hungry. That did not faze me. I knew
how to handle him. The emotional part

of dealing with her, that was the hurt part, that was the part that bothered me the most. I kind of dealt with it a long time. After a while, towards the end of my contract, the last year of my contract, I decided I was sick of her. I was sick of [NAME], I was tired of all of them. And my whole attitude was, "When this job is finished, I will not renew my contract." I knew that was going to be a big deal. I was very well aware of the kind of problems it was going to cause, but I was determined, before I left, I was going to make sure that everything that I set out to do was completed, that the building was up, that it was furnished, that everything was done. The way I ended up deciding to leave, and this may sound very strange to you, (laughs) but the way I started to leave was, there was another woman who also worked for this guy, and she acted as one of the [?? 51:48] coordinators with me with the city. Her

hair was falling out, she was sick all the
time, she was starting to take medicine
all the time, and then I realized I was
starting to have some of her same
symptoms. I decided that was when I
was not with going to renew my contract
any more. I dealt with it pretty good for
a long time, and then I got to a point
where I thought, "This job is just not
worth it, and when my contract is up, I'm
not renewing. I don't care what they say
this time." Last time I did that,
everybody started crying. But not this
time. This time, I thought, "that is
enough."

Participant 9

That's basically what I have been
trained to do all of my adult life and all of
my childhood. You have to adapt; you
have to overcome. I have a belief that
the grass is not always greener on the
other side, not every day is going to be

perfect. There is going to be highs and lows. And you know, I just deal with the lows and hope that there will be other highs in the future. If I succumb and just let this overtake me, then who is lost? I have, ultimately. I refuse to do that to myself; I refuse to do that to my family. I have a light at the end of the tunnel, and I am just keeping in step and watching for that light at the end of the tunnel. One good thing about it, as I am approaching my exit, I just think this has prepared me for the next chapter, because as far as being able to be a little more humble and swallow the big pill and deal with a little more friction, I think this has actually better prepared me for that next step that I am going to take in life, so I will know how to negotiate future obstacles. I take whatever can be thrown at me that is negative, and I just find a way to make it positive.

Participant 25

> Because we were disconnected, and I
> was in a totally separate organization,
> that was a coping mechanism in itself,
> because I did not have to see him every
> day (laughs). That was one part of it.
> The other part of it was, you know, I am
> a godly man, so I prayed, not only for
> him, but I pray for the situation to get
> better, and just prayed for my attitude
> towards my feelings towards him. That
> also helped. And then, also, the nature
> of my job. We traveled a lot. So, (??)
> gone, out of the area. That helped me
> cope with the situation as well.

Lack of Well-Defined Responsibilities

A challenge that some participants expressed
was a lack of well-defined responsibilities. This lack of
codified or verbalized responsibilities seemed to
cause challenges in regard to participants'

expectations. Some participants appreciated the
flexibility, while others desired a more defined role
within the organization. The participants shared the
following statements referencing this theme:

Participant 21

> I started off as, like I said, I started off in
> one job and I moved to another job.
> Eventually, like I said, I ended up being
> the mayor's aide, his press secretary of
> sorts. We found we had a need for the
> minorities in the city and in the city's
> employment, to have somebody to
> come to when they had a problem. That
> was the kind of jump start for the rest of
> these things. We would have, like, for
> instance, you might have somebody that
> called down to City Hall, and they may
> have a complaint about going into the
> neighborhood and it was a primarily
> Caucasian neighborhood and then
> somebody African-American would
> move in, and either they were having a

complaint because of harassment, or
the person whose neighborhood they
were moving into thought it was their
neighborhood and nobody else should
be able to come in to it, you know? That
kind of thing. The reason the alderman
suggested we create that position for
me was because we had policemen who
felt they were being unfairly treated …
and they were. They needed somebody
to dig into it, and after I was assigned
that job to dig into it and find out about
the disparities in training and promotions
and all of that, that's when they decided,
"Okay, we have done that, now we do
not necessarily want her to continue to
do that. We are going to move her out
of that position, and we are going to
make her a Neighborhood Planner." I
go, "Well, what is a Neighborhood
Planner?" "We do not know, figure it out.
This is your job." That Minority Affairs
position no longer existed.

Participant 21

For the Minority Affairs situation, it came
about when there was a complaint.
When you had, for instance, we had,
somebody went to an alderman, he was
one of the police officers and was
complaining about an assistant chief,
and how they were being singled out, or
how they would be calling and their days
off were denied [INAUDIBLE] they could
not get promotions, those kinds of
things. Those kind of things might come
from a call that was made. The other
thing, usually, somebody calls the
mayor's office, they have a problem,
and they just forward all that information
to me, because they did not want to deal
with it. Those kinds of things. Going in
the Neighborhood Planner's part of it,
that came about because, like I said,
they wanted to change my title because
– now, the way they said it was that title

seemed to [imply] we had problems in
our city, and they did not want that to be
the case. It's like changing the name of
a medication when you find out there['s]
something wrong with you. You know
what I'm saying? (laughs). They
changed it to the Neighborhood Planner
and told me to figure out what that was.
And that sort of backfired on them a little
bit, because that gave me an open hand
to deal with everything, everybody in the
department and out of department. I did
– because they did not give me any
guidelines on how I was supposed to do
it, I had the opportunity to do it my way,
and it turned out to be a good
[INAUDIBLE] for us. I do not think you
necessarily wanted that, but, the …
assistant to the mayor, the second
person under the mayor – Chief
Operations Officer, that is who he is. He
did not necessarily like [INAUDIBLE].
He was kind of a racist. He was racist,
he was sexist, and he was former

military, little short guy who had a Napoleonic complex. He had every kind of little stuck-up issue you could think of. I guess he decided, now he was in the South, he could really exercise that. The problem with that was, I was not from the South, and so we sort of bumped heads. That is where a lot of the trouble started.

Participant 25

Yes. The organization actually held several events, and had conferences where they talked about diversity, and brought in a number of organizations that actually came in and they talked about how their particular organization could help identify the diversity within our organization, and also gave some historical background. For example, we had the Native American Indians come in, and they talked about how Native Americans, how they helped America throughout the first establishment of the U.S., and how they were able to help America grow to where they are now. Other organizations talked about the African-American History Month, we talked about the Hispanics Month, and Women's Month, all these different organizations came in and they talked during that one-month period. I think the organization tried to, instead of having a month for every different verse, ethnicity, or organization, they tried to have one month where they had everyone included, and at an all-inclusive time that we could all reflect and get information on whatever the organization was.

Participant 25

Well, the reward and discipline, it could be formal and informal. Of course, the formal is, through our evaluation, we have a once-a-year evaluation. You

would put forth the description on your
job, and the accomplishments of that
job, and then your supervisor would
then so-called evaluate you and put his
evaluation. And in those comments,
that could be looked at as a reward.
They would have to write a separate
letter of recognition, or some type of
reward, if he deemed you needed an
award. That usually came once a year.
If you had some kind of disciplinary
action, that was more immediate
(laughs). You know? If you said
something that he deemed needed to be
corrected or (?? 15:50) military, you (??)
or whatever it is, you are going to have
to be disciplined according to the rules
and regulations for whatever action
needed addressing.

Participant 25

The interaction that we had with him,
like I said, we did not have a weekly

meeting, which I was accustomed to
and used to having. We did not have a
weekly meeting at all. The daily, weekly
interaction was not there, unless a
couple of things happened. What would
cause us to have an interaction was, a
request for information from our higher
headquarters or external agencies. He
would then have to communicate that
information to me, and say, "Hey, I need
you to do X," or whatever. That would
cause communication. And then the
annual appraisal, the performance
appraisal that we would have to do. We
had to have that done on (?? 26:58).
That was a requirement from the higher
military organization we worked for. That
was a requirement for them, so we had
to have that done. But, outside of that,
we did not have a lot of day-to-day
interaction. That, it is what it is.

Synthesis of the Perceptions of African-American Employees in LMX Out-Groups

The overall perception of the African-American employee was a conglomeration of emotions that appeared to manifest from several prominent negative factors in the 12 themes, which dominated the transcripts of the participants. The synthesis of the themes the researcher generated from the participant transcript asserts the existence of negative environments and negative interactions with their respective Caucasian supervisors. The basis of the screening tool was perception, so there is no surprise that there are some negative connotations to stories and encounters.

The most significant theme was the negative supervisor interaction. Participants disclosed a variety of negative interaction with their respective supervisors on a regular basis. They expressed these negative interactions in a variety of ways from very direct and overt confrontation to subversive passive-aggressive actions. Some participants expressed frustration and depression, which was in concert with other themes expressed such as lack of well-defined responsibilities, a negative environment, and lack of communication.

The environment proved a significant factor worth mentioning by participants. Several expressed a culture that likely facilitated the negative integrations or forms of communication. For example, workspaces that were physically separated facilitated communication by e-mail or limited face-to-face communication. Another example of the environmental impact on the leader-member dyad would be the expressed extreme lack of diversity that facilitated feelings of a lack of commitment to inclusiveness by organizational leaders. This theme may be connected to the expressed interpretation of how the supervisors applied policy. Although some participants noted a lack of concerted effort by organization leadership to positively address inclusiveness, some participants perceived purposeful alienation and or exclusion of the African-American employee.

The participants' expressions of a theme of favoritism was in concert with the theme of inconsistent application of policy. Some participants

expressed that leaders did not always apply the same
policy to all in the same manner. Some participants
expressed concerns because of observing fellow
employees receive benefits they were personally
denied. The way the leaders communicated also
manifested this theme.

A common theme was prevalent regarding the
importance of communication to the strength of the
leader-member dyad. It was clear the communication
of the supervisor was limited or lacking in
thoroughness. The feedback on duties left
participants wanting more information and sometimes
confused on expectations. This was akin to the
theme of the lack of well-defined responsibilities and
the overlooking of participant capabilities.

The lack of, or limited communication methods,
seemed to degrade the leaders' understanding of the
abilities (capabilities) of the participants. This limited
communication seems to result in limited duties below
the participants' fullest capabilities and lack of job
satisfaction on behalf of the participants. This limited
communication appears to be present in the
communication of responsibilities.

The participants routinely asserted managers

did not clearly codify or verbally articulate their responsibilities. This left them confused on whether they were satisfactorily completing tasks or meeting expectations. This left some participants to their own devices in determining the parameters of what was considered an acceptable job. Some participants communicated that the frustration resulted in purposely reducing effort and underperforming. This was possibly due to the leadership styles present within the organizations.

Participants characterized laissez-faire leadership, authoritative leadership, and micro-management as the most prevalent leadership styles. There were instances in which they described the supervisors as being continuously removed from providing leadership. In contrast, there were a few instances of micro-management or an authoritative approach that seemed to align with the themes that suggested a lack of appreciation of abilities. The supervisors seemed to exhibit more controlling actions than recognition of the participants' abilities would warrant.

Last, some participants expressed the development of coping mechanisms to deal with the negatively-characterized relationships with their supervisor. Some participants looked inward and addressed the stresses and challenges with spiritual tools such as praying and seeking faith-based solutions. The participants expressed their coping mechanisms as committing deeper to their work, withdrawing, or seeking professional counseling.

Conclusion

This chapter has provided a brief synopsis of the methodology utilized for the execution of this research. It has outlined the detail of the approach the researcher took to data analysis, coding, and thematic analysis. The chapter established the perceptions of the participants by establishing themes through the analysis of the coded interviews. The chapter provided a synthesis of the various themes to give a greater appreciation of the situation of African-American members who exist in the LMX out-group. Chapter 5 provided greater context on the relevance of the data the researcher collected as it relates to the research question: how do African-American subordinate employees within the out-groups of their

Caucasian immediate supervisors, as defined by the
LMX theory, describe their leader-member dyad
narratives?

CHAPTER 5
DISCUSSION, IMPLICATIONS,
AND RECOMMENDATIONS

Introduction

The purpose of this exploratory, qualitative inquiry was to gain a greater understanding of the personal experiences of African-American subordinate employees in the out-groups of the LMX dyadic relationships and to gain insight into how they view themselves and their working relationships. The researcher defined the diverse demographic as the ethnic difference between the manager and the employee. The researcher investigated the perspectives of the African-American subordinate employees in the LMX out-group of Caucasian supervisors and identified factors that enhanced or detracted from the development of the professional relationship.

Summary of the Research Results

The world's workforce continues to grow in diversity due to the globalization of commerce and the transplantation of individuals from their areas of origin. As the demographics of the workforce changed, so does the likelihood that leaders would supervise individuals of a different race or culture. Quantitative research validates the impact of diversity on leadership.

The researcher conducted this qualitative research to address the lack of knowledge of the personal experience of minority employees negatively affected by increased diversity. The researcher explored personal experiences of African-American subordinate employees in the out-group of Caucasian supervisors as defined by the LMX theory. This provides an opportunity to address a gap in the knowledge of a theory of organizational management and leadership: LMX. The gap in the literature is specifically about qualitative research and the lack of personal perspectives of the minority within the LMX theory out-group (Amogbokpa, 2010).

This research is significant to the success of organizations today faced with the increasingly demographically diverse workforce of the United States (Avery et al., 2010). This study may contribute to the more effective management of a diverse employee population by building upon existing management relationship research and expanding LMX theory. This may contribute to the field of organization and management due to the increasing significance of diversity within the global workforce.

The findings may provide leaders with information to improve interactions with their demographically diverse staff. The study focuses on a population of subordinates with experience of being in the out-groups of diverse leader-member dyads. The result may form a foundation upon which researchers can merge social and behavioral science research with leadership studies to achieve more effective and culturally diverse global organizations.

Literature Review

Four decades (1980-2019) highlighted the development of VDL into LMX. The seminal literature focused heavily on the paradigm and research approach, which has shifted since 1980. Maturation has marked the research recognizing major stages, characterized and identified by the normalized metrics scholars have employed. The literature showed evidence of attention to performing quantitative assessments throughout the evolution of LMX. Those quantitative studies focused on positive or high-quality LMX relationships, but paid little attention to the low-quality LMX relationships resulting from membership in the out-groups of the supervisor's workforce.

The research community did not address the gap in the knowledge until recently (circa 2009). The literature reviews highlighted Bolino and Turnley (2009) as leading researchers who addressed this perceived gap in knowledge on out-groups. Bolino and Turnley's model measured how the out-group's perception of LMX status impact attitudes and work behavior.

Although scholars have increased attention to out-group research in recent years, the literature the researcher reviewed remained heavily quantitative in nature and/or limited in scope in qualitative inquiry (Gwynne, 2014; Walker, 2011). The authors of recent

(circa 2011) qualitative studies on LMX continued to
modify the elements they measure to assess the
strength of the leader-member dyad. Gwynne (2014)
focused on low-quality dyads to gain a greater
appreciation for dyad member's negative perceptions
of organizational justice and commitment. Wu (2010)
also found value in gaining understanding of the
perceptions of those in the out-group. Wu conducted
a two-part quantitative study that first measured GNS
– the individual's job fit in correlation to being in the
out-group. The second part of Wu's study reconciled
the GNS with whether an out-group member felt
strongly enough to strive to change their status from
an out-group to an in-group. Wu asserted out-group
members exhibited a strong desire for growth.

Methodology

The research method was qualitative. The
research designs the researcher chose were an
exploratory, qualitative inquiry that utilized purposive
data collection to reduce the participants' perspectives
of the meanings they ascribed to the experience so
the researcher could identify common themes and

present them as research findings (Androff, 2010).
Purposive sampling was necessary because a
specific demographic is critical in successfully
gathering relevant data to address the research
question (Stebbins, 2001).

The researcher collected data until data
saturation was reached via recordings and word
processing documents (Bernard & Ryan, 2010). The
researcher utilized NVivo 10, which imported data
from the documents and assisted with sorting, coding,
categorizing, and inductive analysis of each leader-
member dyad. The researcher utilized NVivo 10to
facilitate adherence to the research process and to
reduce potential researcher bias.

The research question that guided this study
inquired how African-American subordinate
employees within the out-groups of their Caucasian
immediate supervisors, as defined by the LMX theory,
described their leader-member dyad narratives. The
exploratory, qualitative research design the
researcher utilized provided the best parameters and
constructs from which the sample population could
provide data relevant to the research question.

The researcher solicited participation within the

study utilizing a Facebook, LinkedIn, and blog posting. Upon receiving a notification of interest, the researcher sent an e-mail to potential participants, explaining the requirement for completion of the LMX-7 Questionnaire and the Demographics Screening Instrument. The researcher utilized the LMX-7 Questionnaire to identify members of the LMX out-group. The researcher requested and received permission to utilize the LMX-7 Questionnaire.

Upon review of the LMX-7 Questionnaire and Demographics Screening instrument results, the researcher purposively selected a sample of the population to ensure maximum variance. The researcher asked the participants to complete an Informed Consent Form or confirm during the interview. The researcher interviewed those consenting to participation with the questions in Appendix A. Upon receipt of the validated transcripts from the participants, the researcher analyzed the data.

Discussion of the Results

This research study addressed the research question, "How do African-American subordinate employees within the out-groups of their Caucasian immediate supervisors, as defined by the LMX theory, describe their leader-member dyad narratives?" The research study data revealed 12 themes of the African-American subordinate employee narrative. The themes ranged from negative supervisor interaction to perception of the importance of communication to the development of a positive relationship with the supervisor. The researcher reconciled the themes with the conceptual framework, literature review, and research question.

The preponderance of the themes the researcher identified within the research participants' transcripts alluded to environments and encounters wrought with negative attributes. These conditions were in concert with the LMX theoretical framework within this study. The LMX theory asserts the effectiveness of leadership is positively or negatively affected during the maturation of the leader-member dyad (Graen & Uhl-Bien, 1995). The findings of this study highlighted negative aspects of the leader-member dyad, which led to less effective leadership.

The LMX theory framework served as the paradigm by which African-American subordinate employees provided their respective narratives of their personal experiences within the out-group of their immediate supervisors. The researcher gained insight into the characteristics of those less favored within the supervisor purview. The findings provided insight that addressed the gap in the LMX research literature, with emphasis on the personal perspectives of the racial minority within the LMX theory out-group (Amogbokpa, 2010).

The main limitation on the study was the fidelity of data arising from the phone interviews and the researcher's experience in conducting phone interviews. The study design was simple and direct, which limited the potential for flaws in design. The research design had one flaw, which limited the ability to generalize or compare and contrast data from the various research participants. The researcher did not measure the experience level and effectiveness of the supervisors before conducting the interviews. It was assumed the participant's leaders possessed the ability to lead. Through the conduct and content of participant interviews, the researcher noted some supervisors had no experience before the beginning of the leader-member dyad. This research design element could act as a limitation to lateral comparisons of the participants' narratives when significant disparities could exist between supervisors.

Implications of the Study Results

The data analysis identified 12 themes in the responses of the participants. This research supported the assertions that low-quality relationships that developed within the leader-member dyads had negative impacts on individuals within the out-group. Existing literature placed a heavy focus on members within the in-group. Existing contributions identified the benefits of being within the in-group. The findings of this research confirmed the negative impacts of low-quality dyads. The entire sample population was African-American individuals with Caucasian supervisors. There were no direct interview questions related to whether participants felt their race was a factor in them being in the out-groups of their supervisors. The researcher deemed that type of question to be leading, and potentially it could have impacted the rest of the data gathered. The interview question that inquired about factors participants felt yielded negative actions and environment did highlight some feelings that the supervisors' actions were racially motivated. The participants who noted a perception of membership in an out-group, as a result of race, cited the racial composition of the staff and their personal observations of differences in communication and treatment.

This study adds to the existing body of findings that supports the existence of negative attributes of LMX relationships of low quality. This study adds to the body of knowledge on the factors potentially contributing to the existence of low-quality LMX relationships. This study also contributes to the limited known narrative of African-American employees existing in LMX out-groups.

The findings of the study support the existence of negative attributes of being within the out-group characterized by poor communication and strained relationships with leaders as identified in the research

of Graen, Liden, and Hoel (1982) and Pelletier (2012).
The themes that highlighted the importance of
communication and the impact upon participants
when interpersonal communication was ineffective
supported the existing literature on out-groups; the
out-group leaders' and members' interaction would
only encompass actions that organization policy or
practice mandated (Graen, Liden, & Hoel, 1982).

The findings that highlighted the participants'
assertions of emotional and physical negative effects
of the leader-subordinate relationship supports
existing LMX research that purports persistent stress
is an indicator of existing (membership) within the
LMX-out-group (Bond et al., 2010; Hansen et al.,
2006; Meglich-Sespic et al., 2007; Oladapo & Banks,
2013). The existence of stress within the out-group
highlighted a need for participants to develop coping
mechanisms to offset the negative personal impacts.

These findings address the lack of depth of
research into the feelings (emotions) of employees
engaged in (who are members of) low-quality
exchanges with their respective supervisors.
Scholars noted lack of knowledge on the implications
of the attitudes on outgroup members' performance

and the impact on the overall organization (Boies & Howell, 2006; Ford & Seers, 2006; Graen & Uhl-Bien, 1995; Maslyn & Uhl-Bien, 2005; Sparrowe & Liden, 1997)

This research contributes to the body of knowledge within the field of organization and management by presenting findings on the existence of leadership attributes and actions that may contribute to leadership success. Findings contribute to research on the impacts of diversity on leader-member dyads. The study suggests the application of several findings regarding the benefits of quality communication will contribute to the success of leadership within a racially diverse workforce.

This study adds to the field of organization and management by presenting an African-American subordinate out-group narrative that identifies factors a supervisor can address to strengthen the leader-member dyad of demographically diverse workforces. An improvement in leader-member dyad facilitated by the LMX theory literature encourages improvements in the effectiveness of the dyad in addressing organizational objectives. The themes of this research provide potential constructs for further

research to build upon out-group understanding and
the impacts of diversity.

Limitations of the Study

The researcher developed this study with
specific attention to demonstrating the validity of the
research procedures and applying strict discipline to
protocols. The evaluation of the limitations of the
study falls into two categories: researcher experience,
and phone interviews. The researcher's experience
in the interview process was extensive. However,
was new to the use of NVivo software. The
researcher utilized NVivo tutorials software videos to
gain familiarity with the software to mitigate the level
of experience. The use of phone interviews limited the
opportunity to visually observe body language
responses to interview questions. The researcher
utilized probing questions and allowed sufficient time
to allow the participants to expound upon answers to
mitigate the lack of face-to-face interviews.

Recommendations for Further Research

To expand the research on the implications of
diversity for the LMX theory, researchers should
include four additional conceptual frameworks:
leadership quality, additional demographic attributes,
the existence of institutional racism, and the transfer
of power within organizations. Further research will
expound upon and increase the understanding of the
complexities of leading a diverse workforce.
Researchers can address these four conceptual
frameworks aggressively in a single study or by
addressing them in an isolated manner.

An assessment of the quality of leadership
before evaluation of the dyad is critical for
establishing a baseline for reconciling the experiences
of research participants. Future researchers could
attempt to reconcile LMX theory with similar theories
such as postmodern organization theory or critical
race theory to further develop the theoretical
constructs of leadership theory.

Study Conclusions

This study has explored the perceptions of
African-American employee experience within the
LMX out-groups of Caucasian supervisors. It has
identified 12 themes within the narrative of 17 African-
American subordinate employees. The themes
related to many negative interactions with
supervisors, such as leaders' perceptions of the
importance of communication and perceptions of
failures to maximize the full potential of the
subordinate. The themes seem to attribute
management and communication failures to the lack
of strength of the dyad and the participants' existence
in the LMX out-group. Some employees identified a
lack of leadership experience and a lack of defined
responsibilities. One theme among the employees
was frustration with the underestimation of their skills.
Research findings identify themes that provide
insights into leadership characteristics, environment
characteristics, and relational dynamics that may
contribute to leaders leading organizations with
diverse demographics more successfully. The

findings of this study add to the body of knowledge on
organization and management.

REFERENCES

Amabile, T. M., Conti, R., Coon, H., Lazenby, J., & Herron, M. (1996). Assessing the work environment for creativity. *Academy of Management Journal, 39*, 1154-1184. doi:10.2307/256995

Amogbokpa, T. G. (2010). *The connection between the two facets of trust (supervisor trust and subordinate trust) and leader-member exchange relationship in two manufacturing organizations.* Doctoral dissertation, Capella University UMI Number: 3423169

Andresen, M. (2007). Diversity learning, knowledge diversity and inclusion. Theory and practice as exemplified by corporate universities. *Equal Opportunities International, 26*, 743-760.

Androff, D. (2010). "To not hate": Reconciliation among victims of violence and participants of the Greensboro Truth and Reconciliation Commission.

application, and innovation. *Psychological Bulletin, 103*(1), 27-43. doi:10.1037//0033-2909.103.1.27

Available from ProQuest Information & Learning. (Document No.7726747)

Avery, D. R., Lerman, B., & Volpone, S. D. (2010). Investigating the racio-ethnic differences in the link between workplace racio-ethnic dissimilarity and life satisfaction. *Cultural Diversity and Ethnic Minority Psychology, 16*, 307.

Bacharach, S. B. (1989). Organizational theories: Some criteria for evaluation. *Academy of Management Review, 14*, 496-515.

Barge, J. K., & Schlueter, D. W. (1991). Leadership as organizing: A critique of leadership instruments. *Management Communication Quarterly, 4*, 541-570.

Bell, D. A. (1980). *Race, racism, and American law* (2nd ed.). Boston, MA: Little, Brown and Company.

Bernard, H. R., & Ryan, G. W. (2010). *Analyzing qualitative data: Systematic approaches.* Los Angeles, CA: Sage.

Bhal, K. T., Gulati, N., & Ansari, M. A. (2009). Leader-member exchange and subordinate outcomes: Test of a mediation

model. *Leadership & Organization Development Journal,*
30(2), 106.

Blau, P. (1964). *Exchange and power in social life.* New York,
NY: Wiley.

Boies, K. & Howell, J.M. (2006). Leader-member exchange in
teams: An examination of the interaction between
relationship differentiation and mean LMX in explaining
team-level outcomes. *Leadership Quarterly,* Vol. *17,* pp. 246-
247.

Bolino, M. C., & Turnley, W. H. (2009). Relative deprivation among
employees in lower-quality leader-member exchange
relationships. *Leadership Quarterly, 20*(3), 276-286.

Bond, S. A., Tuckey, M. R., & Dollard, M. F. (2010). Psychosocial
safety climate, workplace bullying, and symptoms of
posttraumatic stress. *Organization Development Journal,*
28(1), 37-56. Retrieved from Business Source Complete
database. (48056247)

Braun, V. & Clarke, V. (2006) Using thematic analysis in
psychology. *Qualitative Research in Psychology,* 3 (2). pp.
77-101. ISSN 1478-0887

Byrne, D. (1971). *The attraction paradigm.* New York, NY:
Academic Press.

Cashman, J., Dansereau, F., Graen, G., & Haga, W. J. (1976).
Organizational understructure and leadership: A longitudinal
investigation of the managerial role-making process.
Organizational Behavior and Human Performance, 15(2),
278-296

Contemporary Justice Review, 13(2), 269-285.

Cooper, D.R. & Schindler, P.S. (2008). Business research
methods (10th ed.). New York: McGraw-Hill Irwin.

Copi, I. M. (1954). Essence and accident. *Journal of Philosophy,*
51, 706-719.

Crouch, M. & McKenzie, H. (2006). The logic of small samples in
interview based qualitative research. *Social Science*
Information, 45(4), 483-499.

Culture, leadership and organizations: The Globe study of 62
societies. Thousand Oaks, CA: Sage.

Dansereau, F., Graen, G. B., & Haga, W. (1975). A vertical dyad
linkage approach to leadership in formal organizations.
Organizational Behavior and Human Performance, 13, 46-
78.

de Cremer, D., van Dijke, M., & Bos, A. E. R. (2006). Leader's
procedural justice affecting identification and trust. *Leadership*

& *Organization Development Journal,* 27, 554-565.
doi:10.1108/01437730610692416

Delgado, R. (2000). *Critical race theory: The cutting edge.*
Philadelphia, PA: Temple University Press.

Dienesch, R. M., & Liden, R. C. (1986). Leader-member
exchange model of leadership: A critique and further
development. *Academy of Management Review, 11,* 618-
634. doi:10.5465/AMR.1986.4306242

Dovidio, J. F., Hebl, M. R., Richeson, J. A., & Shelton, J. N.
(2006). Nonverbal communication, race, and intergroup
interaction. In V. L. Manusov & M. L. Patterson (Eds.),
Handbook of nonverbal communication (pp. 481-500).
Thousand Oaks, CA: Sage.

Ford, L. R., & Seers, A. (2006). Relational leadership and team
climates: Pitting differentiation versus agreement. *The
Leadership Quarterly, 17,* 258-270.

Gerstner, C. R., & Day, D. V. (1997). Meta-analytic review of
leader-member exchange theory: Correlates and construct
issues. *Journal of Applied Psychology, 82,* 827-844.
doi:10.1037/0021-9010.82.6.827

Gouldner, A. W. (1960). The norm of reciprocity: A preliminary
statement. *American Sociological Review, 25*(2), 161-178.

Graen, G. B., & Cashman, J. F. (1975). A role-making model of
leadership in formal organizations: A developmental
approach. In J. G. Hunt & L. L. Larson (Eds.), *Leadership
frontiers* (pp. 143-165). Kent, OH: Kent State University
Press.

Graen, G. B., & Ginsburgh, S. (1977). Job resignation as a
function of role orientation and leader acceptance: A
longitudinal investigation of organizational assimilation.
Organizational Behavior and Human Performance, 19(1), 1-
17.

Graen, G. B., & Scandura, T. A. (1987). Toward a psychology of
dyadic organizing.

Graen, G. B., & Schiemann, W. A. (2013). Leadership-motivated
excellence theory: An extension of LMX. *Journal of
Managerial Psychology, 28,* 452-469.

Graen, G. B., & Uhl-Bien, M. (1995). Relationship-based
approach to leadership: Development of leader-member
exchange (LMX) theory of leadership over 25 years:
Applying a multilevel multi-domain perspective. *Leadership
Quarterly, 6,* 219-247.

Graen, G. B., Dansereau, F., Minami, T., & Cashman, J. (1973).

Leadership behaviors as cues to performance evaluation.
Academy of Management Journal, 16, 611-623.

Graen, G. B., Liden, R. C., & Hoel W. (1982). The role of
leadership in the employee withdrawal process. *Journal of
Applied Psychology, 67*, 868-872.

Graen, G. B., Novak, M. A., & Sommercamp, P. (1982). The
effects of leader member exchange and job design on
productivity and job satisfaction: Testing a dual attachment
model. *Organizational Behavior and Human Performance,
30*, 109-131.

Gwynne, J.L. (2014). *The effects of low-quality LMX dyads on
subordinate perceptions of organizational justice and
organizational commitment: A phenomenological
investigation* (Doctoral dissertation). Available from ProQuest
Dissertations and Theses database. (ProQuest Document
ID. 1626367838)

Hansen, Å. M., Hogh, A., Persson, R., Karlson, B., Garde, A. H.,
& Ørbæk, P. (2006). Bullying at work, health outcomes, and
physiological stress response. *Journal of Psychosomatic
Research*, 60(1), 63-72.
doi:10.1016/j.jpsychores.2005.06.078

Hinkin, T. R. (1995). A review of scale development practices in
the study of organizations. *Journal of Management, 21*, 967-
988.

Hofstede, G. H. (1984). The cultural relativity of the quality of life
concept. *Academy of Management Review, 9*, 389-398.

House, R. J., Hanges, P. M., Javidan, M., Dorfman, P., & Gupta,
V. (Eds.) (2004).

Humes, K. R., Jones, N. A., & Ramirez, R. R. (2011). *Overview
of race and Hispanic origin: 2010*. Washington, DC: U.S.
Census Bureau. Retrieved from http://www.census.gov/

Journal of Business Studies Quarterly, 4(4), 107-120. Retrieved
from ProQuest database. (1449792123)

Katz, D., & Kahn, R. L. (1966). *The social psychology of
organizations*. New York, NY: John Wiley & Sons.

Katz, D., & Kahn, R. L. (1978). *The social psychology of
organizations* (2nd ed.). New York, NY: Wiley.

Keller, T., & Dansereau. F. (1995). *LMX: Dyads embedded in
groups or dyads independent of groups?* Paper presented at
the annual meeting of the Academy of Management,
Vancouver, BC, Canada.

Kerr, S., Schriesheim, C. A., Murphy, C. J., & Stogdill, R. M.
(1974). Toward a contingency theory of leadership based

upon the consideration and initiating structure literature. *Organizational Behavior and Human Performance, 12*(1), 62-82.

Klein, K.J., Dansereau, F., & Hall, R.J (1994). Levels issues in theory development, data collection and analysis. *Academy of Management Review*, 19(2), 195-229.

Lapierre, L. M., & Hackett, R. D. (2007). Trait conscientiousness, leader-member exchange, job satisfaction and organizational citizenship behaviour: A test of an integrative model. *Journal of Occupational and Organizational Psychology, 80*, 539-554. doi:10.1348/096317906X154892

Liden, R. C., & Graen, G. (1980). Generalizability of the vertical dyad linkage model of leadership. *Academy of Management Journal (Pre-1986), 23*, 451.

Liden, R. C., & Maslyn, J. M. (1998). Multidimensionality of leader-member exchange: An empirical assessment through scale development. *Journal of Management, 24*(1), 43-72. doi:10.1016/S0149-2063(99)80053-1

Lincoln, Y. S. & Guba, E. G. (1985). *Naturalistic Inquiry*. Thousand Oaks, CA: Sage Publications.

Maslyn, J. M., & Uhl-Bien, M. (2001). Leader-member exchange and its dimensions: effects of self-effort and other's effort on relationship quality. *Journal of Applied Psychology*, 86, 697–708.

Meglich-Sespico, P., Faley, R. H., & Erdos, K. (2007). Relief and redress for targets of workplace bullying. *Employee Responsibilities and Rights Journal*, 19(1), 31-43. doi:10.1007/s10672-006-9030-y

Morse, J.M. (1995) The Significance of Saturation. *Qualitative Health Research*, May 1995 5: 147-149, doi:10.1177/104973239500500201

Moustakas, C. (1994). *Phenomenological research methods*. Thousand Oaks, CA:

Nunally, J. C., & Bernstein, I. H. (1994). *Psychometric theory*. New York, NY: McGraw-Hill.

Oladapo, V., & Banks, L. T. (2013). Management bullies: The effect on employees.

Pelletier, K. L. (2012). Perceptions of and reactions to leader toxicity: Do leader–follower relationships and identification with victim matter? *The Leadership Quarterly*, 23, 412-424.

Pettigrew, T. F., & Tropp, L. R. (2006). A meta-analytic test of intergroup contact theory. *Journal of Personality and Social Psychology, 90*, 751.

Portugal, E., & Yukl, G. (1994). Perspectives on environmental leadership. *Leadership Quarterly, 5*, 271-276.

Redmond, M. R., Mumford, M. D., & Teach, R. (1993). Putting creativity to work: Effects of leader behavior on subordinate creativity. *Organizational Behavior and Human Decision Processes, 55*(1), 120-151.

Research in Organizational Behavior, 9, 175-208.

Richeson, J. A., & Shelton, J. N. (2007). Negotiating interracial interactions costs, consequences, and possibilities. *Current Directions in Psychological Science, 16*, 316-320.

Robson, C. (2002). *Real world research: A resource for social scientists and practitioner researchers* (2nd ed.). Malden, MA: African-Americanwell.

Rousseau, D. M. (1998). LMX meets the psychological contract: Looking inside the African-American box of leader-member exchange. *Monographs in Organizational Behavior and Industrial Relations, 24*, 149-154.

Sage. Mumford, M. D., & Gustafson, S. B. (1988). Creativity syndrome: Integration,

Scandura, J. M. (1977). Structural approach to instructional problems. *American Psychologist, 32*(1), 33.

Scandura, T. A., Graen, G. B., & Novak, M. A. (1986). When managers decide not to decide autocratically: An investigation of leader-member exchange and decision influence. *Journal of Applied Psychology, 71*, 579-584. doi:10.1037/0021-9010.71.4.579

Schiemann, W. A. (1977). *The nature and prediction of organizational communication: A review of the literature and an empirical investigation* (Doctoral dissertation).

Schriesheim, C. A., & Kerr S. (1977). Theories and measures of leadership: A critical appraisal. In J. G. Hunt & L. L. Larson (Eds.), *Leadership: The cutting edge* (pp. 9-45). Carbondale: Southern Illinois University Press.

Schriesheim, C. A., Castro, S. L., & Cogliser, C. C. (1999). Leader-member exchange (LMX) research: A comprehensive review of theory, measurement, and data-analytic practices. *Leadership Quarterly, 10*(1), 63-113. doi:10.1016/S1048-9843(99)80009-5

Schriesheim, C. A., Cogliser, C. C., & Neider, L. L. (1995). Is it "trustworthy"? A multiple-levels-of-analysis reexamination of an Ohio State leadership study, with implications for future research. *Leadership Quarterly, 6*(2), 111-145.

Schriesheim, C. A., Neider, L. L., & Scandura, T. A. (1998). A

within-and between-groups analysis of leader-member
exchange as a correlate of delegation and as a moderator of
delegation relationships with performance and satisfaction.
Academy of Management Journal, 41, 298-318.

Shrestha, L. B., & Heisler, E. J. (2011). *The changing
demographic profile of the United States.* Congressional
Research Service Report for Congress. Washington, DC:
Government Printing Office.

Sparrowe, R.T., & Liden, R. C. (1997). Process and structure in
leader-member exchange. *Academy of Management
Review*, 22, 522-552.

Stebbins, R. A. (2001). *Exploratory research in the social
sciences*. Thousand Oaks, CA: Sage.

subjects of research. Retrieved from
hhs.gov/ohrp/humansubjects/guidance/belmont.html

Taylor, S. J. & Bogdan, R., (1998), "In-depth interviewing", In S J
Taylor & R Bogdan (eds) *Introduction to Qualitative
Research Methods: A Guidebook and Resource* John Wiley
and Sons.

U.S. Census Bureau. (2013, July 8). *Race*. Retrieved from
http://www.census.gov/topics/population/race/about.html

U.S. Department of Health and Human Services. (1979.). *The
Belmont report: Ethical principles and guidelines for the
protection of human*

Vecchio, R. P. (1986). Are you in or out with your boss? Business
Horizons, 29, 76–78.

Walker, M. J. (2011). *Trust factors and the leader-member
exchange relationship in diverse organizations: A
quantitative study* (Doctoral dissertation). Available from
ProQuest Dissertations and Theses database. (UMI No.
916617545)

Weitzel, J. R., & Graen, G. B. (1989). System development
project effectiveness: Problem-solving C. *Decision Sciences,
20*, 507.

Wu, K. (2010) *The dark side of LMX: Variances among out-group
members in growth need and work outcomes* (Doctoral
dissertation). Available from ProQuest Information &
Learning. (Document No. 3461180)

Yammarino, F. J., & Dubinsky, A. J. (1990). Salesperson
performance and managerially controllable factors: An
investigation of individual and work group effects. *Journal of
Management, 16*(1), 87-106.

APPENDIX

APPENDIX A

Interview Questions

Questions (LMX Theory)

1. Describe the organization with which you are currently employed.
2. Describe how your organization ensures diversity and inclusion of workforce.
3. Describe your responsibilities within your organization.
   - Describe how your supervisor assigns the tasks of your job.
   - How many of your peers/coworkers work for the same supervisor?
4. Describe the interactions you have with your immediate supervisor.
   - Describe the interactions the supervisor has with all individuals subordinate to him.
5. Describe your supervisor's leadership style.
   - What are the factors you believe influence the leadership style he or she uses with you?
   - (if coworkers) How does he or she apply his or her leadership style to all?
6. Describe the reward and discipline system within your organization.
   - What process is in place to ensure equity in the application of the awards and discipline process?
7. Describe how you feel you make contributions to this organization.
   - How does the organization recognize you and

others for those contributions to the achievement of the objectives of the organization?

8. What do you feel is your responsibility for the relationship that has developed between you and your supervisor?

9. What organization procedures or processes are in place that control or shape the relationship you have with your supervisor?

10. How do you cope with the current situation in your job?

11. What would you do differently if you were to have an opportunity to reestablish your relationship with your supervisor?

12. How would you describe the impact the relationship with your supervisor has on your productivity, job satisfaction, and motivation?

Closeout Question

• Denotes probing questions

INDEX

CURRICULUM VITAE

Larry D. Parker, Jr., Ph.D.
Tampa, Florida
ldparkerjr@gmail.com

TEACHING PHILOSPHY

The teaching philosophy I embrace is the result of over 24 years as an active student-practitioner in the fields of business, management, logistics and leadership. As I reflect on my beliefs regarding teaching and learning, I find that my mission as a teacher is threefold:

• to facilitate a relevant learning experience;
• to create an environment that fosters creative freedom and ability to grow intellectually;
• to inspire to actively participate in defining their learning experience.

To accomplish this, I enjoy applying a wide variety of strategies based on sound learning theory, teaching philosophy and assessments.

Learning theory: The approach to developing the learning experience within my classes is based upon the Andragogy in Practice Model's three dimensions: goals and purposes for learning, individual and situational differences and core adult learning principles.

From my personal experience in management, I develop learning objectives and goals for my courses which are relevant for later use in the workplace. As an alumna of both a traditional and online universities, I recognize the variance in situation and circumstances of the learners. The tasks and assessments used to achieve the objectives in my classes are selected using the andragogy core principles as a guide. Although the education environment is changing greatly due to the expansive reach of technology, the use of the andragogy in practice model also prepares me to be responsive to the needs of a culturally diverse learner class. I respect the difference in perspectives of all my students and encourage them to share to enrich the learning of others.

Teaching Philosophy: The nature of adult learning is unique due to the motivation of the learners. My philosophy of teaching is based upon facilitation theory. I fully embrace the basic premise of this theory requiring the educator to establish an atmosphere in which learners feel comfortable to consider new ideas and not threatened by external factors. I feel true learning occurs when learners can let down their conceptual guard and become open to new paradigms and competing views. They are most likely to build upon their previous knowledge in this situation. I believe in the characteristics of the facilitation theory that suggest that human beings have natural eagerness to learn and that as an educator I am apt to listen to constructive feedback on my teaching methods. I also believe in building relationship with the students that give me greater insight into the unique their respective learning styles.

Assessment: I strongly believe in employing numerous forms of tools to accurately assess understanding of course concepts among learners with a variety of learning capacities. I use rubrics, projects, discussion questions, presentations and or traditional exams/test to ensure learners have mastery of concepts.

By embracing these theories, I have grown into an educator with the desire to continually hewn my craft and share my love for learning by teaching. Thus, I hope to tap into the passions of the learners and inspire them to also become lifelong learners in the pursuit of their academic and professional goals.

TEACHING EXPERIENCE

Program Director, Transportation Logistics Management and Supply Chain Management
2018 - present
American Public University System
Charles Town, WV

Contributing Faculty
College of Management and Technology
2017 – 2018
Walden, University, Minneapolis, MN
Current Course: DBA Chair

- Guide / facilitate researcher completing proposal and research in fulfillment of requirements for a Doctorate of Business Administration

Instructor
Ken Blanchard College of Business
2010 – 2017
Grand Canyon University, Phoenix, AZ

Course: *Action Research Project (PSC 495)*

- Taught non-traditional adult learners online a structured way for managers to take an overview and general management perspective.
- Facilitate student learning through discussion, analysis examination, critical thinking, and real-life experiences. Emphasis focused on a research project that synthesizes major elements of the professional studies program.

Course: *Leading as a General Manager (LDR 620)*

- Instruct non-traditional online students in understanding Prepare leaders for the cross-functional complexities inherent in organizational life.
- Assist students in developing an advanced skill set enabling effective leadership in each of the major organizational functions (marketing, finance, human resource management, information systems, and operations management).
- Explore methods for students to evaluate alternatives to make effective decisions.

Instructor
Central Texas College, Killeen, TX
2009 – 2010

Course: *Principles of Management (BMGT 1327)*

- Instructed non-traditional business students on the various theories and processes of management.
- Identified roles of leadership in business.
- Recognized elements of the communication

process and the guidelines for organizational design.
- Interpreted interpersonal roles related to work groups.

Course: *Business Principles (BUSI 1301)*

- Taught non-traditional college students on a brick-and-mortar campus the concepts concerning the system of business in the United States, to include social responsibility of businesses, business ethics, legal forms of business ownership, and entrepreneurship.
- Facilitate student learning by describing how to build an effective organization and understanding the importance of human relations in the work place. Further, demonstrating an understanding of human resources and production, labor management relations, operations management, financial management and how to manage human resources.
- Ignite student participation by discussing marketing management, product and pricing strategies, distribution strategies, and promotion strategies.

Instructor (Joint Warfighting Center)
2005 – 2008
Joint Forces Command, Suffolk, VA

Course: *Senior Leadership Seminars (Capstone and Keystone)*

- Developed and presented academic seminars for Senior Executive leaders within Department of Defense and State.

- Served on a team that traveled to various locations in the world to facilitate organizational training.
- Tailored presentations routinely to fit the audience and critique their processes during exercises.

MILITARY EXPERIENCE

Deputy, Inspector General (Lt. Col.)
2016 – present
United States Marine Corps, Quantico, VA

- Principal advisor to the Commander and Inspector General of the Marine Corps. Ensuring policy and standards are maintained throughout the organization.

Senior Logistician (Lt. Col.)
2014 – 2016
Central Command
United States Marine Corps Tampa, FL

- Facilitated Marine Corps logistics supply chain management throughout the Middle East.

Program Liaison Officer (Major)
HQs / Equal Opportunity / Diversity Branch
United States Marine Corps, Quantico, VA
2011 – 2014

Course: Marine Corps Leadership Seminar

- Facilitated Marine Corps leadership and ethics training with university students and influencer in their communities.

Commanding Officer / Executive Officer / Operations Officer (Major)
Combat Logistics Regiment – 17

2008 – 2011
United States Marine Corps, Camp Pendleton, CA

- Facilitated team synergy by maintaining lines of communication between staff members. Managed the daily efforts of over 290 people in logistics and maintenance functions.

Observer / Trainer (Major)
2005 – 2008
United States Marine Corps, US Joint Forces Command, Norfolk, VA

- Developed/tailored and presented academic seminars for Senior Executive leaders within Department of Defense and State.
- Served on a team that traveled to various locations in the world to facilitate organizational training.
- Tailored presentations routinely to fit the audience and critique their processes during exercises.

Weapons Project Officer (Major)
2002 – 2005
United States Marine Corps, Marine Corps Logistics Base, Albany, GA

- Supervised operations of >$90 million Amphibious Assault Vehicle upgrade team comprised of government contractors and two departments of defense agencies.

- Facilitated team synergy by maintaining lines of communication between organizations. Managed the daily efforts of over 40 people in logistics functions.
- Coordinated and managed the movement of over $20 million in equipment from the United States to Japan.
- Maintained in-transit visibility of shipments during entire process.
- Developed procedures for the deployment of civilian contractors and military personnel to sites in the Middle East and Far East.
- Wrote and maintained standard operating procedures for the movement of equipment and personnel in support of global war on terrorism from strategic locations around the world to the required destinations.
- Provided operational updates to military leaders and congressional staff, utilizing all forms of Microsoft office software.

Supply Officer (Lieutenant to Captain)
1995 – 2002
United States Marine Corps Air Station, Iwakuni, Japan

- Supervised six Japanese employees in the performance of logistics and supply functions for the United States Marine Corps for three years.
- Able to speak Japanese functionally.
- Coordinated the logistical support of United States foreign military sales.

ENTREPRENEURSHIP EXPERIENCE

President
2014 – present
P42 Trucking LLC, Dallas, TX

- Provide transportation and logistics services in southern region of the United States.

President
1992 – present
PKR Services, Suffolk, VA

- Develop business plans, incorporate businesses, marketing plans, proposal/bid writing, web site development and graphic design.
- Provide small business consulting services.
- Create custom sportswear business.

PRESENTATIONS

- 2018, Diversity and Inclusion Panel, Defense Equal Opportunity Management Institute (DEOMI)
- 2011, Command Climate and Diversity with the Marine Corps – Presented to 100+ new commanders within the Marine Corps, Commander's Course, Quantico, VA
- 2007 – 2008, Joint Task Force Update – Presented to four members of the Joint Staff at the Pentagon, Washington, DC
- 2007, Joint Task Force Sourcing – Presented to 50+ Participants at the FY09 Joint Individual Augmentee Sourcing Conference, Norfolk, VA

- 2006, Building a Joint Task Force – Presented to 15+ Participants at the Capstone and Keystone Conference, Suffolk, VA

EDUCATION

2016, **Ph.D. in Organization and Management,** Specialization: **Leadership,** Capella University, Minneapolis, MN; Dissertation Title: The Impact of Ethnic Diversity in the Workplace: An Exploratory, Qualitative Inquiry on the Experience of Black American Employees in LMX Out-Groups

2006, **Master of Business Administration,** Liberty University, Lynchburg, VA

1995, **Bachelor of Arts in History,** Wittenberg University, Springfield, OH

ABOUT THE AUTHOR

Larry D. Parker, Jr., Ph.D.

Dr. Parker earned his Bachelor of Arts in History from Wittenberg University (OH; 1995), and his Master of Business Administration from Liberty University (VA; 2006), and completed his Doctorate of Philosophy in Organization and Management from Cappella University (MN; 2016). He currently serves as Program Director of Transportation and Logistics Management, and Supply Chain Management within the School of Business, American Public University Systems. In this position, Dr. Parker leads a team of faculty in the delivery of world-class instruction of logistics and supply chain management.

Dr. Parker served as Contributing Faculty and Doctor of Business Administration Chair at Walden University where he mentored doctoral candidates conducting research for solutions to complex, real world business problems. Through research and mentorship, his students built advanced decision making skills.

Dr. Parker is Adjunct Faculty, ADEN University and teaches Leading a Global Team and Personal and Managerial Leadership, in addition to teaching skills that facilitate successful leadership in a dynamic global business environment.

A consummate entrepreneur, Dr. Parker began his first ventures in business ownership as a young man raised in central Texas. He started with payment collections for newspaper routes, advanced to a lawn care business, and ultimately had a complete custom sportswear business before graduating college. He had an unyielding desire to operate his own business and make a difference in his community.

Dr. Parker leveraged over 20 years of business experience into P42 Consulting, which is a management consulting and inspirational speaking company. In 2014, Dr. Parker launched P42 Trucking LLC, a sub-contracted trucking company, operating throughout the southern gulf-coast region of the United States.

SOCIAL MEDIA CONTACT

Email: ldparkerjr@gmail.com

Connect to him on LinkedIn:
https://www.linkedin.com/in/larry-parker1/

Any business-related links or websites you want to
add?

ABOUT THE BOOK

Leaders within organizations must consistently improve their management skills to adapt to the current social and economic environment. As demographic diversity within the workforce grows, from global expansion of organizations, management must develop the skills to meet the challenges and advantages such diversity presents.

This is an absolute read for every leader, supervisor, and manager. All leaders should be interested in honing their skills to match the workplace environment of today and the future. This book also provides a tool for diversity and inclusion professionals that desire to research tools to support their assertions made during training or consulting organizations.

This book stresses the value of communications and the potential loss in effectiveness of employees if they are not properly engaged by their leadership. The best time to read this book is in the initial stage of a managerial or supervisory experience. This is applicable to all industries. This is a great tool for any professional within the diversity and inclusion field.

The lessons in this research study also are applicable to life. The value in communication and appreciation of the values of others.

The contents of this book emphasize the value of quality relationships and communication. Future researchers must continue to expand upon qualitative research to further appreciate the dynamics beyond quantitative trends. The qualitative data will give further insight to tangible actions for leaders.

www.ingramcontent.com/pod-product-compliance
Lightning Source LLC
Chambersburg PA
CBHW060449280326
41933CB00014B/2712